1.75

BANKING POLICY AND THE PRICE LEVEL

BANKING POLICY AND THE PRICE LEVEL

AN ESSAY IN THE THEORY OF THE TRADE CYCLE

BY

D. H. ROBERTSON, M.A.

FELLOW OF TRINITY COLLEGE, CAMBRIDGE
READER IN ECONOMICS IN THE UNIVERSITY OF CAMBRIDGE

"She's in that state of mind," said the White Queen, "that she wants to deny *something*—only she doesn't know what to deny!"
"A nasty, vicious temper," the Red Queen remarked.
Through the Looking-Glass.

Third impression, revised

LONDON
P. S. KING & SON, LTD.
ORCHARD HOUSE, 14 GREAT SMITH STREET
WESTMINSTER

1932

First published . . . January 1926
Second impression . . August 1926
Third impression (revised) . . May 1932

PRINTED IN GREAT BRITAIN

NOTE TO 1932 IMPRESSION

A REPRINT of this book has been called for at a time when I am unready to undertake a thorough revision in the light of the criticisms that it has received and of the immense amount of important work on monetary theory that has been elicited by the events of recent years. Since some of the ideas expressed in this book have won interest and approval, I am unwilling to let it go out of print; but I do not know when I shall feel capable of re-writing it or incorporating parts of it in a larger work. In the circumstances I have compromised by making some necessary alterations on p. 58, and re-writing the Appendix to Chapter V in a form which I hope removes some of its errors and obscurities. But I should like to make it plain that in this as well as other parts of the book there is still much with which I am far from satisfied. In particular, the definitions and analyses of Chapter V were worked out for a society of small entrepreneurs, i.e. one in which all incomes are speedily responsive to movements of prices. Reflection and discussion have shown me that they will not stand without modification for a society in which the incomes of most of the factors of production are assumed fixed (or comparatively so), those of entrepreneurs alone being completely mobile.

D. H. R.

CONTENTS

CHAP.		PAGE
I.	INTRODUCTORY	1
II.	APPROPRIATE FLUCTUATIONS OF OUTPUT	6
III.	THE WAGE AND MONEY SYSTEMS	19
IV.	INAPPROPRIATE FLUCTUATIONS OF OUTPUT	34
V.	THE KINDS OF SAVING	40
VI.	SHORT LACKING IN THE TRADE CYCLE	71
VII.	THE RELATIONS OF SHORT AND LONG LACKING	84

CHAPTER I

INTRODUCTORY

§ 1

OF the many attempts which have been made to explain the phenomenon known as the Trade Cycle, there are two which appear at the present time to be commanding an ever-increasing measure of assent. According to the one, the main cause of trouble is to be found in the defects of our monetary system; according to the other, in defects in the judgment and temperament of the leaders of the business world. It seems to me clear that there is a great deal to be said for both of these explanations: but I have never been able to give unqualified assent to either of them, or to any combination of the two. I suspect that the minds of some modern writers are unduly influenced by certain exceptional features of the great post-war boom and slump: I hold that far more weight must be attached than it is now fashionable to attach to certain *real*, as opposed to monetary or psychological, causes of fluctuation: and I am glad to be able to appeal to the pronouncement of Professor Cassel that—

" as long as there is a will to progress, and as long as the material conditions of the satisfaction of this desire require a large use of fixed capital, we must expect a fluctuation in the productive activity of the community akin to the present trade cycles."[1]

Adherents of the "monetary" theory of the trade cycle appear to regard the instability of industrial output as almost exclusively the result, and a plainly undesirable result, of instability in the general price-level. According to the extreme exponents of this theory, "the trade cycle is a *purely* monetary phenomenon."[2] More moderate advocates concede that initial disturbances in the price-level may be due to non-monetary causes, but urge nevertheless that they can and should be counteracted by monetary means.[3]

It will be suggested, on the other hand, in the following pages, first, that there occur important fluctuations in industrial output which are *relatively* desirable, in the sense that, while we can conceive an ideal society in which their causes would be eliminated, those causes are deeply embedded in the technical and legal structure of our actual society; and the remedy, even if practicable, might be worse than the disease. Secondly, that these causes must be expected to produce their effects, whatever monetary policy is adopted. And thirdly, that owing to certain features of our financial system, and those *not* the features against which monetary reformers direct their criticism, this instability of industrial output can hardly fail to

[1] *Theory of Social Economy*, p. 623. I have substituted "trade cycles" for the translator's "conjuncture-movements."
[2] Hawtrey, *Monetary Reconstruction*, p. 141.
[3] See Keynes, *Monetary Reform*, p. 38.

Introductory

be accompanied, as a general rule, by a certain instability in the level of general prices.

Adherents of the " psychological " theory of the trade cycle differ in the weight which they assign both to monetary and to other outside causes; but they are agreed that " the kernel of the explanation is that optimistic error and pessimistic error, when discovered, give birth to one another in an endless chain." [1] In this book I shall have occasion to emphasize that certain variations in the scale of industrial output, whether or not they are socially beneficial, are at least dictated by the self-interest of those who decide upon putting them into force. I do not think it is even nearly true that if all business men always made, and acted upon, true judgments about their own self-interest, industrial fluctuation of a fairly rhythmical character would disappear.

My differences with the dominant schools of thought are therefore partly differences of analysis and partly differences of emphasis. But I am anxious not to overstate these differences, and I have tried at appropriate points of my argument to indicate, even though briefly, my appreciation of the importance of Error, and of the partial Remediability of Error by monetary manipulation. I hold strongly that both a nearer approach to stability of general prices and a wider diffusion of knowledge and common-sense than we have been accustomed to in the past are both possible and desirable; but I suspect that we shall be compelled

[1] Pigou, *Economics of Welfare* (1st edition), p. 848.

to dig more deeply still in our search for the causes and the cures (or rather, the practicable palliatives) of industrial fluctuation. I believe firmly in a policy of " credit-control " as contrasted with a policy of *laissez-faire* in monetary affairs ; but I conjecture that for a long while to come credit-control may prove a more difficult matter than some of its more ardent advocates would lead one to suppose, and that it may have to be envisaged ultimately not as an independent panacea but as one ingredient in a much more arduous and comprehensive programme of Stabilization.

§ 2

The practitioners of most sciences are permitted by public opinion to speak to one another in their own jargon : of economists alone it is apparently expected that their conclusions should be expressed in a form which can be understood without effort by the most general reader. I do not think this expectation is reasonable, and I have made no attempt to fulfil it. This is a difficult book : by expanding it greatly I might perhaps have made it rather less difficult, but not much. I can only plead that it is comparatively short, and implore any reader who is sufficiently interested to read it at all to read each chapter *twice* before proceeding to the next.

The book may also offend in another respect—that it is highly abstract and theoretical. Occasionally, but not often, I have tried to bring out the relevance of an analytical argument by concrete illustration. The book is not intended to be a comprehensive treatise but a theoretical skeleton; and I want the bare bones to stand out strongly.

Chapters II, III, IV and VII are in large part a restatement and development of part of the analytical framework of my *Study of Industrial Fluctuation*, published in 1916, and now out of print. I must repeat my acknowledgment of a special obligation to Prof. Aftalion's *Les Crises périodiques de surproduction*. The present book, and especially Chapter V with its emphasis on the distinction between *material capital* and the *activity of saving*, owes a great deal to Professor Cassel's *Theory of Social Economy*. The important aspect of the trade cycle examined in Chapter VII is illuminatingly discussed in a little-known pamphlet, *Autour de la crise américaine de 1907*, by M. Marcel Labordère, as well as by Cassel and (so far as I can judge without reading the original) by Spiethoff.

I have had so many discussions with Mr. J. M. Keynes on the subject-matter of Chapters V and VI, and have re-written them so drastically at his suggestion, that I think neither of us now knows how much of the ideas therein contained is his and how much is mine. I should like to, but cannot, find a form of words which would adequately express my debt without seeming to commit him to opinions which he does not hold. I have made a few specific acknowledgments in footnotes: happily there is the less need for meticulous disentanglement as his own version of the Theory of Credit is to be published very soon.

CHAPTER II

APPROPRIATE FLUCTUATIONS OF OUTPUT

§ 1

THE most obvious external manifestations of the trade cycle, and the most generally accepted indices of its course, are a quasi-rhythmical movement in the level of prices, in the level of money profits, and in the level of employment. It is not at first sight so clear that these movements imply even a roughly corresponding movement in the volume of production and of consumption. The evidence, however, seems to show that they do, and that the most important phenomenon which we have to attempt to explain is a quasi-rhythmical fluctuation in the real income of the community under consideration. There are, however, certain qualifications to be made. In the first place the volume of *agricultural* production, while it may exercise an important influence on the volume of industrial production, is itself directly subject to influences which, whether or not they are rhythmical in character, are at any rate peculiar to itself: it is therefore on the volume of *industrial* production in the narrower sense (though including therein the output of extractive industry—mining, etc.) that

Appropriate Fluctuations of Output

we must concentrate attention. Secondly, there is in some cycles, though not apparently in all, a marked difference in behaviour between the output of construction goods and the output of goods for immediate consumption. Broadly speaking, it may be said that while the former always declines during the depression below the level attained in the preceding boom, the latter may remain stationary or even continue to advance [1] : so that as regards consumption goods, at all events, the essence of "depression" is not always so much an actual decline of output as a failure to sustain output at the level which, having regard to the existing equipment of productive instruments, is physically possible. Thirdly, there is evidence that in the latter stages of the "boom" of prices, production may cease to make significant advance, while in the latter stages of "depression" of prices production may make a marked recovery.

§ 2

Such then is the behaviour of the volume of industrial output for which a theory of the trade cycle must attempt to account. It will assist us towards constructing such a theory to imagine, as a first approximation, that the conduct of each industry is in the hands of a group of equal co-partners, owning its own instruments of production in common, and deciding in some democratic

[1] Cf. Cassel, *Theory of Social Economy*, pp. 522–8.

manner on its industrial policy, somewhat as is advocated by the theorists of Guild Socialism. This will enable us to ignore for the present any possible divergence between the interests of "Capital" and "Labour," and to ignore also (as is reasonable in connection with the short-period changes with which we are dealing [1]) the possibility of wholesale migration of producers from one industry to another. We need not, however, assume that each industry is "integrated," i.e. that all the stages in the production of any given finished article are in the hands of a single industrial group. We shall reason for the present as though the processes of exchange were conducted without the aid of money by direct barter. On these suppositions let us analyse the reasons for which any one of these industrial groups may find it advantageous now to increase and now to diminish the scale of its output—illustrating our reasoning from such phenomena of real life as do not appear to be inconsistent with our simplified hypothesis, and leaving such as do for later explanation.

It seems that any one of the three following circumstances may offer a rational incentive to an industrial group to alter the scale of its output: (1) an alteration in its real operating costs; (2) an alteration in the intensity of its desire for the goods which it receives in exchange for its products; (3) an alteration in the "real demand price" for its products, that is, in the rate at which other

[1] Pigou, *Economics of Welfare* (1st edition), p. 816.

industries are prepared to part with their products in exchange for its own.

(1) A lowering of its real operating costs will increase the output which it is worth the while of the group to produce,[1] and a raising of real costs will have the opposite effect. Such variations may occur independently in particular industries owing to specific inventions, etc.; but it seems clear that in real life they also occur more or less simultaneously in all industries in association with the phases of the trade cycle. During the later stages of a " depression " there is, generally speaking, a progressive advance in the effectiveness of labour, a progressive overhauling of methods of technique and organization, a progressive writing off of inflated capital charges.[2] During the later stages of a " boom " there is a progressive recourse to inferior instruments of production, a progressive utilization of over-tired labour, wasteful methods of management, and inferior business leadership. The rhythmical nature of these movements does not of course prove that they are an independent and originating cause of the cyclical variations of industrial output; but the automatic and self-

[1] It may or may not increase the aggregate of effort which it is worth its while to expend.

[2] The conception of real cost is a complicated and elusive one, which cannot be thoroughly explored here. It might seem at first sight that an increased effectiveness, due to an increased physical intensity, of labour implies an *increase* of real cost; but if it is accompanied, as in fact it seems to be, by a downward revaluation of the pleasure of idleness, this is not the case. A writing off of capital charges does not, of course, really obliterate the real costs therein crystallized, but it makes them irrelevant to future output.

generating character of the rhythm suggests that it is not unreasonable to suppose that they are.[1]

§ 3

(2) Alterations in the intensity of the desire of any group for the products which it purchases will alter in the same direction the amount of effort which it is worth its while to expend, and therefore its output. Alterations in the intensity of the desire for particular articles are of course continually taking place owing to changes in taste and fashion ; but we are concerned only with alterations so general, and at the same time so intermittent, that they may plausibly be supposed to have some bearing on the course of the trade cycle. Now there is no reason why the intensity of the desire for perishable goods in general—goods, that is, which are consumed in a single act—should alter in any such manner. But with durable goods it is different, for the intensity of the desire for currently produced durable goods depends largely on the quantity of such goods already in the possession of users. This is true even of durable *consumable* goods : it is natural, for instance, that after the brisk demand of the Indian ryot for braziers in 1910,[2] or of the American public for motor-cars in 1922-3, the intensity of the desire for these articles should fall away. But it is even more true, and more important, as regards the instruments of production.

[1] See esp. Mitchell, *Business Cycles*, pp. 475-9, 563-5 ; and Aftalion, *Les Crises périodiques de surproduction*, Vol. II, p. 228.
[2] *Review of Indian Trade*, 1911-12, p. 19.

Appropriate Fluctuations of Output

Thus, as has often been pointed out, if 10 per cent. of cotton-spinning machinery is normally replaced every year, an increase of 10 per cent. in the annual demand for cotton-yarn will warrant in the first year an increase of 100 per cent. in the output of cotton-spinning machinery, to be followed, however, in subsequent years by a relapse to nearly the old level.

Again, the application over a wide field of territory or of industry of an invention such as the railway, electric power, or the Diesel engine, will raise for a more or less prolonged period the intensity of the desire for the constructional implements and materials involved, only to lower it again when the field in question has reached a condition of temporary saturation.[1] The same result will follow from the destruction in any year of an unusually large proportion of the instruments of production in any trade, whether this be as it were the echo of an unusually large construction of such instruments in some previous year, or the result of abnormal incidents such as a San Francisco fire, a German submarine campaign, or a Tokio earthquake.

Again, the intensity of the desire for new instruments depends partly on the expected cost of operating them. Thus a fall in the real operating costs of any of our industrial groups will not only exercise a direct influence in increasing its output

[1] The international boom of 1872 is, in my view, to be particularly connected with railway-building; that of 1882 with inventions in the steel trade; those of 1900 and 1907 with electricity; that of 1912 with oil-power.

12 Banking Policy and the Price Level

(§ 2), but will exercise a further indirect influence in the same direction by increasing the intensity of the desire of its members to acquire new instruments, and consequently the efforts they are prepared to make to acquire them : while a rise in real operating costs will have the opposite effect.[1]

In our hypothetical world, therefore, we should expect the intensity of the desire of any industrial group for instruments, and therefore its output, to be subject to variation : and we should expect some of the causes of variation to occur simultaneously in a sufficient number of industrial groups to produce some variation in an index of the output of the non-instrument-making groups taken as a whole. We should not however expect this variation to be very large ; for in the first place the expenditure of these groups on instruments is a minor part of their total expenditure, and in the second place their desire for the other goods which they purchase may be assumed to be not easily satiable ; and these are factors tending to reduce the increase (or decrease) in the *total* output of an industrial group which will ensue on an increase (or decrease) in its expenditure on instruments.[2] The variations in the output of the

---

[1] As argued in effect by Lavington, *The Trade Cycle*, p. 57.
[2] Along OX measure of units of output by an individual group, along OY measure units of utility derived from the sale of output. cc' = cost curve, uu' = curve of utility of consumable goods purchased by the group. Then if, owing to a decline in the utility-schedule of instruments (not shown in the diagrams), output devoted to purchasing instruments is reduced from OA

Appropriate Fluctuations of Output

instrument-making trades themselves (see below, § 5) will be much larger. This is in accordance with the evidence (§ 1) as to the relative magnitude of the fluctuations in the output of trades making constructional and consumable goods respectively.

§ 4

(3) The effects upon a group's output of an alteration in the real demand price for its products depends upon whether the elasticity of the group's demand for the commodities offered in exchange is greater or less than unity. If the former, a rise in the real demand price for its products will furnish a rational inducement to expand output and a fall to restrict it: if the latter, the reverse will be the case.

to OA_1, uu' is displaced to u_1u_1', and total output is reduced from OB to OB_1. In Fig. 1 $\frac{OA}{OB}$ is large and uu' steep, and BB_1 therefore relatively large; in Fig. 2 $\frac{OA}{OB}$ is small, and uu' flat, and BB_1 therefore relatively small.

FIG. 1. FIG. 2.

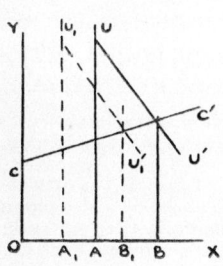
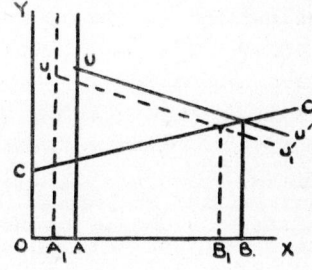

There are three possible causes of such an alteration in real price which require separate mention.

(i) The first is an alteration in the volume of agricultural production, due to a variation in the bounty of nature. The evidence seems to show that normally a decline in the real price of agricultural produce will stimulate industrial output, and an advance will check it; but that a sudden or violent swing in either direction may encounter an inelastic demand, and exercise therefore precisely the opposite effect.

There is still a good deal of disagreement as to whether any rhythm of agricultural production exists, and if so, what it is. Some may be able to swallow Professor H. C. Moore's ingenious demonstration of the existence of an eight-year period in almost all human affairs, depending ultimately on the behaviour of the planet Venus [1]: others will consider that even Professor Pigou's conclusion, that there exists "sufficient regularity to afford the basis of a more or less loose rhythm" [2] goes too far. To the present writer it seems fairly plain, first, that such agricultural periods, if they exist, do not furnish a complete explanation of the periodicity of industrial output; but, secondly, that alterations in the volume of agricultural output often exercise a decisive influence in determining both the *time* at which the various phases of the trade cycle occur and the *magnitude* which they attain.

[1] *Generating Economic Cycles, passim.*
[2] *Op. cit.*, p. 826.

Appropriate Fluctuations of Output

The normal effect of an alteration of the ratio of interchange between agricultural and industrial products is well illustrated in Professor Bowley's well-known table of the price in successive years of British imports in terms of British exports. This table shows minima in the boom years 1890 and 1900, and a marked increase in the depression 1874–7. A continuation of the figures by Mr. Keynes shows a fall in the boom 1905–7 and a rise in the period of hesitation 1908–10.[1]

The abnormal result which ensues when the demand of industrialists for agricultural products becomes inelastic is equally well illustrated by a similar table for the post-war years:

	Export price of imports (average of quarterly figures).	Index of production (average of quarterly figures of London and Cambridge Economic Service).
1913	100	100
1919	87	—
1920	80	100
1921	71	68
1922	76·5	81
1923	79	89
1924	82	91
1925 (first 9 months)	83	87

In 1920–1 there was an abundance of raw products, whose production had been relatively undisturbed by the war, and for which the Russian and Central European markets were practically closed: while "industrial production had been gravely dislocated and its fruits were in keen

[1] *Economic Journal*, December, 1923, p. 477.

demand for reconstruction and re-stocking purposes."[1] The over-violent alteration of the ratio of interchange in favour of industrialists must be set down as one of the leading causes of the slump in the output of British industry.[2] Conversely, the gradual recovery of output from the depths of 1921 is associated with a gradual worsening of the ratio of interchange. During the latter part of 1924 something like a true equilibrium of relative prices was for a time established; and the sharp rise in those months of the prices of certain raw products, notably wheat and wool, seems to have been, while it lasted, a factor favourable to the recovery of British industrial output.

§ 5

(ii) A second possible cause of an altered real demand price for the products of an industrial group is an alteration, in the opposite direction, in the operating costs of some other industrial group. If we assume that the demand of each group for the products of every other is normally elastic, it follows that the decline of real costs during "depression" and their advance during "boom" need not themselves be universal in order to generate in one case a universal expansion, in the other case a universal contraction, of output.

---

[1] See article by the present writer in *Economic Journal*, 1924, pp. 286 ff.

[2] An instructive parallel is afforded by the effect of "excessive" world wheat crops in intensifying the reaction in trade in the United States and United Kingdom in 1883-4 (cf. H. S. Jevons, *Causes of Unemployment*, p. 69).

An alteration in relative prices does not therefore necessarily mean that one industrial group is prospering at the expense of another: it may, according to circumstances, indicate a situation in which both have a rational inducement to expand, or a situation in which both have a rational inducement to contract, their output. In particular a lowering of the cost of production of basic constructional materials may constitute a rational incentive to the expansion of output on the part of pretty nearly every trade.[1]

It must not, however, be assumed that the demand of each industrial group for the products of every other is invariably elastic. In particular there are two important groups of industries—those producing instruments and those producing the service of transport—for whose products in time of depression the demand is likely to be highly inelastic: in the former case because, for reasons discussed in § 3, the demand has already reached something like saturation-point; in the latter case because there is at any time a clear physical limit to the quantity of goods requiring transportation. A further increase of output and reduction of real price by these industries is likely therefore not to stimulate but to check an expansion of output on

---

[1] An invention which lowers constructional costs does not bring its own Nemesis as does an invention which enhances the effectiveness of finished instruments (§ 3). Contrast the mildness of the reaction in Germany from the boom of 1882, which was due to the cheapening of steel production by the basic process, with the severity of the relapse in the same country from the boom of 1900, due mainly to the electrification of the means of transport and illumination.

the part of other industries. This consideration suggests that the loud clamours heard during depression, in the alleged interests of an increase of general industrial activity, for indefinite reductions in railway rates and in constructional costs, may be mistaken.

(iii) A third cause of an altered real demand-price for the products of a group is an alteration in the intensity of the desire for those products. The reasons for which alterations may occur in the intensity of the desire for instruments have already been discussed in § 3; it remains only to add that such alterations must be expected to generate not only *moderate* alterations in the output of the groups which produce consumable goods, but relatively *large* alterations, of a quasi-rhythmical character, in the output of the groups which produce instruments.

The general conclusion thus is that even in the simplified industrial world which we have constructed we should not expect the appropriate or optimum rate of industrial output to be constant, but to be subject to a succession of what may be called " justifiable " increases and decreases, some at least of which are of a fairly rhythmical nature.

CHAPTER III

THE WAGE AND MONEY SYSTEMS

§ 1

WE must now begin to bring our analysis into closer accord with real life by gradually taking into account some of the actual features of our wage and monetary systems.

In the actual world, decisions about the scale of output and about the purchase of new instruments are made, not by co-operative groups, but by the members of a relatively rich employing class, who hire the services of relatively poor wage-earners and give them orders which can on the whole be effectively enforced. It is accordingly possible that the changes in output dictated by the self-interest of the employer, and successfully enforced by him, should differ in magnitude from those which would be dictated by the self-interest either of the actual workman or of our hypothetical " group-member "; and there are several reasons for supposing that in fact they are considerably greater than the former and somewhat greater than the latter.

In the first place the demand, in terms of effort, of the typical employer for income in general is likely to be more elastic than that of the workman, at any rate for the short periods of time with which we are concerned. When trade is good the employer, owing to the more exciting and pleasurable nature of his work, is readier than the workman to expand his expenditure of effort : he is also, owing to his sophisticated tastes, better placed than the workman for expanding his consumption. When trade is bad he is, owing to his comfortable circumstances and his addiction to gentlemanly pursuits such as golf and politics, readier even than the workman who is assured of full employment, and far readier than the workman who is threatened or visited with the loss of his job, to contract both his effort and his consumption. We may suppose the elasticity of demand for income of the hypothetical group-member to be intermediate between that of the actual employer and that of the actual workman ; since he would share neither the privileged position of the former nor the precarious status of the latter.

Secondly, it is to the employer alone that alterations in the cost (Chap. II, § 5) and in the technical efficiency (Chap. II, § 3) of productive instruments are of direct importance ; and the consequent changes in the output of the trades making consumable goods are likely therefore to be greater than the immediate self-interest of the workman in these trades would dictate. They are likely also to be somewhat greater than under a regime of co-operative groups : since the proportion of total

The Wage and Money Systems 21

income expended on instruments[1] is likely to be greater in the case of the typical employer than in the case of the typical group-member.

Thirdly, our monetary system, as is well known, operates so as to reduce real wages and certain other charges in the early stages of an expansion of output, and to increase them in the early stages of a contraction of output; and these changes exert the same influence on the output-policy of the employer as though they were not mere transferences of income, but changes in real cost (Chap. II, § 2).[2]

For these reasons there is ambiguity as to what exactly we are to mean by the appropriate or optimum rate of industrial output. Are we to mean the rate dictated by the self-interest of employers, or of workmen, or of hypothetical beings in whose persons the divergent interests of the two are reconciled? The first will in all probability be subject to considerably greater variation than the second, and somewhat greater variation than the third. That the manual workers are cajoled and lectured into overwork in time of boom, and condemned to walk the streets in search of employment in time of depression, does not *necessarily* prove that errors of judgment are being committed by the employing class: it might only argue a dis-

---

[1] $\frac{OA}{OB}$ in the figure, p. 13.

[2] Further, changes in the physical intensity of labour and capital readjustments at the expense of external investors (cf. p. 9 n.) present themselves as unequivocal alterations in cost to the employer.

harmony of interest between "Capital" and "Labour" more real and fundamental than most of those to which the critics of our social order have directed their attention.

It may indeed be urged that in this matter of industrial stability, as in certain other matters, the ultimate divergence of interest between the employing and employed classes is less than the immediate divergence. It has yet to be proved that a community in which the *immediate* interest of the manual worker is made the sole criterion of economic policy is safe from industrial stagnation or decay. And unless and until society acquires a complete technical control over the explosive forces of industrial progress, it may well be that the ultimate interest even of the wage-earning class as a whole is best served by a measure of industrial instability. I do not feel confident that a policy which, in the pursuit of stability of prices, output and employment, had nipped in the bud the English railway boom of the forties, or the American railway boom of 1869–71, or the German electrical boom of the nineties, would have been on the balance beneficial to the populations concerned. At all events, for the remainder of this study, I shall speak of a change in the scale of output which would commend itself to the enlightened self-interest of the employing class as a "justifiable" change. But it must not be forgotten that the change is only "justifiable," and the resulting scale of output is only the "appropriate" or "optimum" scale, *relatively* to the existing organization of society,

The Wage and Money Systems 23

and to its existing powers of control over the forces of technical progress.

§ 2

We must next take into direct account the fact that exchanges are made not by barter, but with the aid of money. We shall find that while the *results* of the causes of change classified in Chapter II are correctly expressed by making the hypothesis of direct barter,[1] the chain of motives brought into play by a monetary economy is different, and the results are reached in part by a different route.

We shall return for the present to the assumption that our industrial groups consist of equal co-partners of similar incomes and tastes. We shall assume that the Government or banking authority has power to inject money at some point into the industrial system; and we are bound to assume further that these monetary injections are not free gifts, but are made by way of loan. But we shall ignore at present the *time-element* in these loans, and regard them solely in their aspect as currency issues.

Let us suppose then that there are only two

[1] As is commonly done nowadays even in non-academic discussions of the problems of international trade.

Pigou (*Economics of Welfare* (1st edition), p. 818) asserts as self-evident the identity of the two processes. "A change in the output of agriculturalists is seen, or expected, by industrialists to involve a change in the aggregate amount of money which will be paid to agriculturalists, and which agriculturalists can, therefore, afford to offer for the products of industrialists, thus making it to the interest of industrialists to alter correspondingly their own output. This is, of course, merely a roundabout way of saying that industrialists will be ready to create an altered amount of their products . . . in return for an altered amount of agricultural products."

commodities, wheat and iron, of each of which there is an annual exchangeable output of 100 units, exchanged by means of a monetary stock of £100 : each unit of this stock changes hands twice a year, and the price, both of a unit of wheat and of a unit of iron, is £1. Now let us suppose that owing to a reduction in real costs—caused, say, by an agricultural invention or an increase in the kindliness of nature—the annual output of wheat is increased to 150 units ; and let us suppose that the elasticity, in terms of effort, of the iron-makers for wheat is such that under a regime of barter their output would be increased to 120 units, and the iron-price of wheat become $\frac{4}{5}$, or the wheat-price of iron $\frac{5}{4}$. We have to inquire by what route and with what price-accompaniments this result will be reached under a monetary system.

The answer seems to depend on the policy adopted by the monetary authority. Among the many policies open to it we may select four as having some kind of logical basis, and exhibit in tabular form the new position of equilibrium which would result from each. We may assume the existence of a class of wheat-merchants who form a convenient point for the injection into the system of any increased supplies of money which the monetary authority may see fit to provide. By the term "impact price," employed below, is meant the price first established when the stream of money is directed on to the commodity in question, and before the consequent reaction, if any, on its output has had time to occur.

	Money value of output. £	Total quantity of money. £	"Impact price." £	Equilibrium price. £	"General price-level" (arithmetic average).
(a) Money-supply unaltered.					
Wheat	100 }	100	{ $\frac{2}{3}$	$\frac{2}{3}$ }	$\frac{3}{4}$
Iron	100 }		{ 1	$\frac{5}{6}$ }	
(b) Money-supply adjusted so as to reflect the effort-elasticity of demand. (See below, § 3.)					
Wheat	120 }	120	{ $\frac{4}{5}$	$\frac{4}{5}$ }	$\frac{9}{10}$
Iron	120 }		{ $1\frac{1}{5}$	1 }	
(c) Money-supply adjusted so as to preserve ultimate stability of general price-level.					
Wheat	$133\frac{1}{3}$ }	$133\frac{1}{3}$	{ $\frac{8}{9}$	$\frac{8}{9}$ }	1
Iron	$133\frac{1}{3}$ }		{ $1\frac{1}{3}$	$1\frac{1}{9}$ }	
(d) Money-supply adjusted so as to keep the price of wheat unaltered.					
Wheat	150 }	150	{ 1	1 }	$1\frac{1}{8}$
Iron	150 }		{ $1\frac{1}{2}$	$1\frac{1}{4}$ }	

With policy (a), the incentive to increased iron output is clothed entirely in the form of a reduction of wheat-prices, that is (we may say), in the cost of living. With (b) and (c) it is clothed partly in this form and partly in the form of an increased stream of money-demand for iron, causing a temporary rise of price until output is appropriately adjusted, and a permanent increase in the stream of money directed by iron-makers towards the purchase of wheat. Under (d) it is clothed entirely in this latter form.

§ 3

With a pliant monetary system, ready to follow the line of least resistance, it seems that (b) is the policy most likely to be adopted. For if the underlying elasticity, in terms of effort, of the iron-group for wheat is as stated, the monetary *symptom* of this condition will be that, if wheat-merchants attempt to get rid in some short period of time of some stated *small* fraction, n, of the annual wheat-output, they will, now that the wheat-output has been increased, have to submit to a reduction in price to £$\frac{4}{5}$, and will find their money receipts increased by $\frac{1}{5}$.[1] They will therefore regard £$\frac{4}{5}$ as the "natural" price of wheat under the new conditions, and will requisition the monetary authority for sufficient money to take over the whole of the increased output at that price.

While (b) is thus in a sense the most "natural" policy, it would not perhaps much matter, if the iron-producing group really consisted of equal co-partners, which of the four policies were adopted. But if we now assume, as in § 1, the existence of our actual wage-system, it becomes probable that (d) is the most *effective* policy for establishing the appropriate output, or failing (d), (c), (b) or (a), in that order of preference. The reason is that, under our existing wage-and-money system, a more direct and immediate stimulus to increased output is afforded by rising money receipts than by falling

[1] This proposition is the only method of bringing together the conceptions of "real" and "money" elasticities of demand that I can devise. It is, I suspect, implicit in the sentences of Pigou quoted on p. 23, n. 1. The fraction n must be small, because we are to suppose that the money-receipts of iron-makers have not yet been increased: it would therefore be impossible, if n were large, for their real elasticity of demand to symbolize itself in the way supposed.

prices of the objects of expenditure. The employer is likely to pay more attention to rising money profits than to a lowered " cost of living " for himself, or to the possibility of reducing money wages owing to the lowered cost of living of his workmen. The workman who is standing out of employment to protect his standard of life is much more likely to suffer himself to be absorbed in consequence of a rise in money wages than in consequence of a fall in the cost of living; and even the employed workman is likely to be more sensitive to the former process.

Of the four monetary policies, therefore, (d) seems likely to be the most effective in producing the required result, while (b) combines moderate effectiveness with a certain naturalness and theoretical attraction. From neither point of view is (c), the policy aiming at ultimate stability of the general price-level, at the top of the poll. Moreover, even (c) involves a *temporary* rise in the price of iron sufficient to produce a *temporary* rise in the " general price-level."

§ 4

When we have to deal with more than two commodities, the situation is, of course, more complicated; for the increased expenditure of wheat-consumers on wheat will be partially but not wholly compensated by a diminished expenditure on other things. If the money-supply is increased, probably some producers (e.g. of iron) will be specially favoured by the increased money demand of the wheat-growers, while others (e.g. of boots) will find that there is a reduced money demand for their product from those who are now spending more money on wheat, which is not compensated for by an increased money demand either from wheat-growers or from iron-makers; and will be induced, therefore, to restrict output. Others, again, may find themselves enriched in money, but having no desire to purchase wheat, may find that the prices of the things which they do desire to purchase have risen against them in about an equal degree; so that they will have on the balance no *rational* inducement to alter their output. It is impossible for any eye to follow the ramifications of the forces generated by the additional output of wheat. It is only by retaining a firm grasp of the implications of the term " elasticity of demand " that we can infer that whatever the monetary policy, the inducements to expand output must on the balance exceed the inducements to contract it; and it is only with the aid of reasoning of the type employed in Chapter II, § 3, that we can discuss the magnitude of this excess. Thus we can say that it will be greater the greater the elasticity of supply in non-wheat industries (e.g. the more unused plant and labour they have in reserve when the change takes place), and the less the elasticity of their demand for each other's products (i.e. the more reluctant they are to curtail their miscellaneous consumption). The monetary routes by which these results are reached are not, I think, possible to visualize in detail. The relative merits, however, of the various possible monetary policies would seem to remain the same as in the simpler case discussed in § 2.

A similar line of argument can be followed in cases when, demand for a product being elastic, a rise in its real costs stimulates a curtailment of output on the part of other industries : and in cases when, the demand for a product being inelastic, a fall in its real costs stimulates a contraction and a rise in its real costs stimulates an expansion of output on the part of other industries.

§ 5

The monetary interpretation of the type of change discussed in Chapter II, § 3, is somewhat more complicated. Let us suppose first that there are only two commodities, machines and "consumables," of each of which there is an annual exchangeable output of 100 units, exchanged by means of a monetary stock of £100 : each unit of this stock changes hands twice a year, and the price both of a machine and of a consumable is £1. Now suppose that, owing to an invention, the desire of consumable-makers to acquire machines expands, so that they would, under a system of barter, be willing to offer 140 consumables for 100 machines, or 150 consumables for 120 machines : and that this latter rate of interchange is satisfactory also to machine-makers, so that the new appropriate annual rate of output will be 120 machines and 150 consumables.

The initial monetary signal of the changed state of affairs is that consumable-makers (their money incomes being at present unchanged) are prepared to offer $n \times £140$ instead of $n \times £100$ for $n \times 100$ machines, where n is some *small* fraction. The subsequent developments depend on the policy adopted by the monetary authority in respect of its currency-issues to machine-merchants, and may be tabulated as follows:

	Money value of output. £	Total quantity of money. £	"Impact price." £	Equilibrium price. £	"General price-level."
(a) Money-supply unaltered.					
Machines	100 }	100	{ 1	$\frac{5}{6}$ }	$\frac{3}{4}$
Consumables	100 }		1	$\frac{2}{3}$ }	
(b) Money-supply adjusted so as to reflect change in real demand for machines.					
Machines	140 }	140	{ $1\frac{2}{5}$	$1\frac{1}{6}$ }	$1\frac{1}{20}$
Consumables	140 }		$1\frac{2}{5}$	$\frac{14}{15}$ }	
(c) Money-supply adjusted so as to preserve ultimate stability of general price-level.					
Machines	$120 \times 1\frac{1}{9} = 133\frac{1}{3}$ }	$133\frac{1}{3}$	{ $\frac{133\frac{1}{3}}{100} = 1\frac{1}{3}$	$1\frac{1}{9}$ }	1
Consumables	$150 \times \frac{8}{9} = 133\frac{1}{3}$ }		$\frac{133\frac{1}{3}}{100} = 1\frac{1}{3}$	$\frac{8}{9}$ }	
(d) Money-supply adjusted as described below.					
Machines	> 150 }	> 150	{ $> 1\frac{1}{2}$	$> 1\frac{1}{4}$ }	$> 1\frac{1}{8}$
Consumables	> 150 }		$> 1\frac{1}{2}$	> 1 }	

Under policy (*a*), the stimulus to consumable-makers is clothed entirely in the form of a direct impulse to expend more effort in order to acquire a given quantity of money. After the collapse of the initial monetary signal described above (a signal which policy (*a*) prevents from being permanently displayed), the stimulus to machine-makers is clothed entirely in the form of a reduced money cost of consumables. Policy (*a*) is thus a very ineffective route for attaining the appropriate output.

The "natural" policy of a pliant monetary system is probably (*b*), under which sufficient purchasing-power is put into the hands of machine-merchants to enable them to purchase the whole current output of machines at the price established by the initial jerk of the money demand of consumable makers. Under both (*b*) and (*c*) the stimulus to increased output is felt by both groups partly in the form of an increased stream of monetary demand; but it is also felt partly, by machine-makers in the form of a lowered price of consumables, and by consumable-makers in the form of a direct impulse to expend more effort in order to acquire a given quantity of money.

For the stimulus to both groups to be felt entirely in the most effective form of an increased stream of monetary demand, some policy of the type (*d*) must be adopted. The minimum necessary expansion of the money-supply depends upon the elasticity, in terms of money, of the supply of consumables. Even if this elasticity were infinitely great, the requisite expansion of the money-supply would, in our particular case, be 50 per cent.; and if we are entitled to assume that that elasticity is not infinitely great, the requisite expansion of the money-supply must in fact be greater than 50 per cent.[1]

---

[1] The diagram represents the supply conditions of consumables in terms of money. P is the original point of equilibrium, so that OM = 100, MP = £1. The essence of policy (*d*) is that the

§ 6

Thus in this case also a policy aiming at ultimate stability of the general price-level seems to be neither the "most natural" nor the "most effective" policy for the monetary authority to adopt. The superiority in effectiveness of policy (*d*) is, however, under a wage-system, not so great in this case as in the case discussed in §§ 2–4; for in this case the "non-monetary" motive, i.e. the increased desirability of machines, acts directly upon the minds of the entrepreneurs in charge of production, whereas in the previous case we saw that the "non-monetary" motive, i.e. the lowered price of wheat, acts chiefly upon the minds of the workmen who have no direct control over output policy. The case for a policy of price-stability is therefore rather stronger in the present than in the previous connection. Even such a policy, however, involves

supply-curve must not be lowered, the whole stimulus to the expansion of output from OM to ON (ON = 150) coming in the

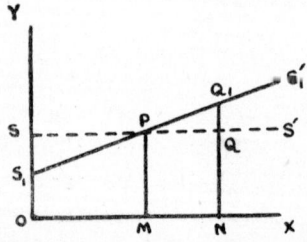

form of a raising of the demand-curve (not shown). If SS′ were horizontal, NQ would = £1, and ON × NQ (i.e. the total money-supply) would = £150. But if we are entitled to assume that in the short period SS′ slopes upwards, as $S_1S_1′$, NQ_1 must be > £1, and ON × NQ_1 must be > £150.

The Wage and Money Systems

a temporary rise in the price, first of machines, and later of consumables.

When we take into account the existence of numbers of different kinds of consumables, the monetary routes by which equilibrium is reached become, as in the parallel case discussed in § 4, too complicated for the eye to follow in detail. Suppose, for instance, the initial change to consist in an increased desire on the part of shipowners to possess ships; then the motor-trade, for instance, may be adversely affected on the balance owing to a diminished stream of monetary demand from shipowners, while the boot-trade, for instance, may be favourably affected on the balance owing to an increased stream of monetary demand from shipyard workers. All we can say is that there will be an increase in the appropriate scale of output for the consumable trades taken as a whole, but that this increase will be less than the increase in the appropriate volume of consumables purchased by machine-makers.

CHAPTER IV

INAPPROPRIATE FLUCTUATIONS OF OUTPUT

§ 1

THE main suggestion of Chapter II was that in the economic world as we know it, rational and justifiable fluctuations of output must be expected to occur. The main suggestion of Chapter III was that the moving causes of these fluctuations inevitably involve an initial disturbance of the general price-level, and that a monetary policy designed to restore it to its original figure is neither the most natural response of the monetary system, nor the most effective in interpreting the underlying situation and establishing the results for which it calls. This suggestion will be reinforced when we come to take account of the fact that production takes *time* and requires the aid of *saving*, and of the manner in which this fact is intertwined with our monetary system.

Meanwhile, it is necessary, in order to avoid misconception, to discuss briefly the reasons for which the *actual* fluctuations in industrial output tend greatly to exceed the rational or appropriate fluctuations hitherto examined.

The first step in this discussion is to call attention

to a fresh ambiguity in the conception of an appropriate or optimum scale of industrial output (cf. also Chap. III, § 1). This ambiguity arises from three closely-allied facts, all rooted in a single technical characteristic of modern industry—the necessity in many trades of using very large, expensive, and durable instruments of production.

The first fact is that when the instrument of production is very large, the process of investment in the trade concerned is imperfectly divisible. The underlying economic situation may justify an increase in productive capacity of 50 per cent. ; but technical considerations may impose a decision between 100 per cent. and nothing. A railway company, for instance, must either double its track or not double it : it is of no use to lay a third rail. It follows that the optimum expansion of industrial output *relatively* to the exigencies of the technical situation may be much greater than the expansion of output which would be really appropriate in view of the underlying conditions of utility and cost.

The second fact is that in many trades a large part of the costs are, as it were, crystallized in these durable instruments. In face, therefore, of a situation calling for a decline of output, the producer has to decide not what it would be his interest to do if he had a clean sheet as regards production costs, but what it *is* his interest to do having regard to the supplementary costs to which he stands committed. If producers in all other trades are in the same position, so that in spite of an increase in his output the terms of exchange will not turn in his disfavour, or if, even though the terms of exchange turn in his disfavour, the demand for his products is elastic, then he may find an advantage in actually increasing output instead of diminishing it, since by so doing he may diminish the sum by which his total receipts fall short of his total costs.[1] Thus the rate of output which is best relatively to the existing situation is greater than the best rate of output that we can conceive.

[1] Along OX measure units of output, along OY units of *aggregate* real costs and receipts. OA = curve of aggregate receipts —which, to illustrate the case in which the terms of exchange will not alter whatever the output (since all other producers are

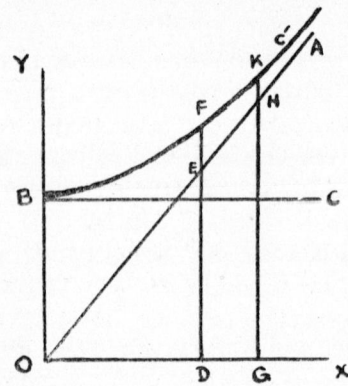

in the same position), is drawn as a straight line. BC = curve of supplementary costs, BC′ = curve of aggregate prime costs (assumed to increase more than in proportion to output) measured from BC as base.

Then an increase in output from OD to OG will diminish net loss from EF to HK.

The third fact is that in many cases the durable instruments of production are *intractable*. It costs money to lay up a ship or to damp down a blast furnace, while to leave a coal-pit unworked may lead to flooding and collapse. In all such cases the best rate of output, having regard to the costs, immediate and deferred, of putting the instrument out of commission, is greater than the rate of output which would be best if no such costs existed.

It is partly for such reasons as these that the output of ordinary consumable goods does not, as a rule, fall off during a depression of trade to the extent which the theoretical arguments of Chapter II might lead us to expect.

§ 2

The main reason for which the actual expansions of industrial output which occur are greater even than the *relatively* most appropriate expansions, seems to be the stress of competition, aggravated by the length of time which is required to adjust production to a changed demand. If the conditions are such that our hypothetical producing-group (Chap. II) would be furnished with a rational inducement to a 10 per cent. increase of output, but if, in fact, the trade is organized into fifty independent and competing firms, it is quite likely that each firm, regarding itself as the special protégé of Providence, and ignorant of the preparations that are being made by its neighbours, will prepare to provide, say, one-twentieth instead of its appropriate one-fiftieth of the appropriate total increase in output, so that total output is increased by 25 per cent. instead of by 10 per cent. The demands of each firm for new instruments of production will be correspondingly exaggerated, and the longer the new instruments take to construct, the more scope there is for miscalculation, and the greater will be the excess of the actual output of instruments over the output which is really appropriate to the situation. The more severe, too, will be the restriction ultimately necessary, both in the original trade and in the instrument-making trades, to bring the rate of output down to the appropriate level; or, alternatively, the greater will be the divergence between the rate of output which remains relatively best and that which would be ideally best (§ 1).[1]

§ 3

The remaining causes of divergence between actual and appropriate output must be briefly dismissed here, not because they are not of very great importance, but because they have been so often and so thoroughly discussed. In the first place—

"apart altogether from the financial ties by which different business men are bound together, there exists among them a certain measure of psychological interdependence. A change of tone in one part of the business world diffuses itself, in a quite unreasoning manner, over other and wholly disconnected parts."[2]

[1] The importance of the principles discussed in these two sections is illustrated in some detail in my *Study of Industrial Fluctuation*, Part I, Chapters 1 and 2.

[2] Pigou, *Economics of Welfare* (1st edition), p. 840. See the whole chapter in which these sentences occur: and Lavington's *The Trade Cycle, passim*.

Secondly, so far as the inducements to a producer to expand (or contract) output are clothed in the form of an increased (or diminished) stream of money demand, they are in many cases partly illusory; for the rise (or fall) in price turns out not to be confined to the product which he sells, but to affect also in greater or less degree the products which he buys. Hence, the alterations actually made in the scale of output tend to exceed the appropriate alterations; hence also that monetary policy which is most effective in bringing about quickly and without friction the appropriate alteration will also tend to overshoot the mark, and to be, unless kept well in control, the most fertile in the generation of error.

The aim of monetary policy should surely be not to prevent all fluctuations in the general price-level, but to permit those which are necessary to the establishment of appropriate alterations in output and to repress those which tend to carry the alterations in output beyond the appropriate point. The importance of this distinction will become still plainer when we come to examine more closely the *time*-element in production and the nature of a modern monetary system. To that task we must now turn.

CHAPTER V

THE KINDS OF SAVING

§ 1

In order to make progress, it is necessary at this point to undertake an inquiry, much of which inevitably covers familiar ground, into the nature of the thing called Capital and the activity called Saving. This can most conveniently be done by establishing certain distinctions, which assist towards clearness of thought.

(1) In the first place we must distinguish between the activity of providing Capital and the material goods, if any, towards the provision of which that activity is directed. The essence of the activity of providing capital has long been recognized to lie in an abstention from immediate enjoyment of consumable goods which it has become customary to call "Waiting." This term, however, carries a suggestion of voluntary postponement of benefits to be some day enjoyed which will be found hampering in our present discussion. The older term, "Abstinence," while free from the suggestion of future benefit, imparts a flavour of moral struggle and merit which has rightly led to its rejection. "Going without"

bears the right shade of meaning, but is clumsy: I propose, for want of a better, to employ the almost equally colourless word "Lacking."

A man is lacking if during a given period he consumes less than the value of his current economic output. This is not always the same thing, as we shall see later, as spending on immediate consumption less than his legal money income during the period. If during a given period a man consumes more than the value of his current economic output, he may be said to be dis-lacking. The amount of Lacking done in a given period may be measured by the volume of consumable goods lacked, or perhaps more satisfactorily by the number of days' labour of a given quality whose product is lacked, during that period. The things in the provision of which Lacking eventuates I propose to call Capital. Lacking which has been done in the past is crystallized in the stock of Capital existing at the present moment.

§ 2

(2) The second distinction to be drawn is between Fixed, Circulating, and Imaginary Capital, and between their correlative activities, which may be called respectively Long, Short, and Unproductive Lacking. Long Lacking is directed towards providing society with the use—of necessity slow and gradual—of the fixed and durable instruments of production : Short Lacking towards enabling society to carry on production—including the production of durable instruments—by methods which

are technically efficient, but slow and indirect. There is thus little ambiguity about the nature of Fixed Capital: it consists of factories, railways, machinery, and so forth. But about the nature of Circulating Capital some dispute has arisen. Modern economists rightly warn us [1] against adopting the view, countenanced by Adam Smith and Jevons, that such capital consists mainly in stocks of goods available for immediate consumption by workpeople and others engaged in the dilatory processes of production; for since production in all branches of industry is carried on simultaneously, there is no reason why in a well-ordered community, even though it employs very long and indirect methods of production, such stocks should attain any very great dimensions. Nevertheless, Circulating Capital does consist of real goods—not, however, of finished goods only, but of a shifting congeries of goods in all stages of their passage from the soil to the ultimate user or consumer; but it comprises also some goods—such as coal used in industry—which never reach the consumer's hands at all, and some—such as the crop for which the ground has been prepared but which has not yet been sown—which it takes the eye of faith to see.

The origin of the opinion that Circulating Capital consists mainly of stocks of consumable goods is to be sought in the fact that, to bring any lump of Circulating Capital to the stage which it has reached, the expenditure of labour of various kinds has been

[1] See Cassel, *Theory of Social Economy*, p. 38; Henderson, *Supply and Demand*, p. 124.

necessary, and those who performed this labour have had to be accorded a real income of consumable goods. Thus the essence of Short Lacking is seen to lie in some persons going without consumable goods in such wise that other persons, who are engaged in a lengthy productive process, consume them.

The value of the Circulating Capital in a " steady " community (i.e. one which is either stationary or progressing at a uniform rate) bears to the total annual output of goods a relation depending on the length, and also on the character, of the average period of production of goods—that is, the length of time which elapses between the date at which their production is taken in hand and the date at which they reach the hands of consumers. If the process of production is absolutely even, i.e. if during it the goods increase in value at a uniform rate, the value of the Circulating Capital is equal to half the value of the goods produced during a production-period—e.g. if the production-period is a year, the Circulating Capital is equal to six months' output. If, however, the goods grow more rapidly in value during the earlier stages of production, as is seen to be likely when we reflect that the " production-period " includes the time during which finished goods are merely being held in warehouses and shops, the Circulating Capital is equal in value to something between one-half and the whole of the output during a production-period.

While the identity of the goods in which Circulating Capital consists is constantly changing, the total outstanding supply of such Capital in a "steady" community must itself be "steady." This is nearly true even with regard to goods, such as wheat, whose production, in the narrow sense, is subject to seasonal variation, since in a steady community the consumption of the final products into which they enter is presumably evened throughout the year, so that the total amount of Short Lacking required by the whole chain of trades involved is approximately steady. Even in a "steady" community, however, we should scarcely expect the requirements of *each individual business* for Short Lacking to be steady ; nor again should we expect constancy in the proportion between the Short Lacking which those who direct the business are able and willing at any moment to provide themselves, and that for which they are impelled to have recourse to outsiders. Hence, in practice we find that congealed Short Lacking is continually being released by some entrepreneurs and absorbed by others. In an unsteady community this fact has important consequences, as we shall see : but it is important to realize that a mere transfer of this kind does not involve the provision of any *new* Lacking, and also that, as applied to the total supply of congealed Short Lacking, the word "Short" does not imply any presumption that the Lacking will speedily, or indeed ever, be released.

It remains to add a word about Unproductive Lacking. New Unproductive Lacking consists in going without goods in favour of persons who wish to anticipate their incomes, but are not engaged in expanding the production of generally marketable commodities. The most important form of Unproductive Lacking in modern times consists in the transfer of spending-power to Governments, mainly for the prosecution of war. We may say, if we like, that such Lacking is immediately cancelled by equivalent Dis-lacking on the part of the borrower, and does not result in the provision of Capital at all. But it may also be convenient to say that it results in the provision of Imaginary Capital, since the paper securities sometimes given in receipt for it, while they represent no store of material goods of any kind,[1] may be said to represent, in favourable circumstances, the immaterial wealth of national security or prestige.

§ 3

(3) The third distinction to be drawn is between what we may call Applied Lacking and Abortive Lacking or Hoarding; and again, within the former category, between Lacking applied directly and Lacking applied indirectly. Suppose a man to acquire a sum of money in exchange for the sale of part of his current output. If he uses his money-claim in the purchase of an instrument, or in making advances to productive workers, he may be said to be applying Lacking directly to the provision of Capital. If he hands his money-claim over to

---

[1] This statement is not formally accurate, since *at some stage* in its history, part of this Lacking is represented by half-finished munitions, stocks of blankets, etc. But the great mass of such Lacking outstanding at any moment is not so represented.

another person who uses it for the provision of Capital, he may be said to be applying Lacking indirectly. If, however, he neither presents his money-claim himself nor hands it over to another, but simply adds it to his existing money stocks, he may be said to be Hoarding, or more strictly performing New Hoarding. In this case he is from his own point of view saving, but is taking no steps to ensure the creation of Capital. Unless others take such steps, the effect of his action, assuming equilibrium of production and sale to be preserved, is that the consumption of other persons is increased by as much as his own consumption is diminished.

We may, if we like, speak of the total amount of Real Hoarding outstanding at any time, and say that it equals the value, in terms of goods, of the money of all kinds in circulation. And we can go on to point out that the magnitude of this amount depends on the habits and preferences of the public, and bears, in the case of each individual, some fairly definite though not unchangeable relation to his real capital wealth or his real annual income or a combination of the two.[1] But we must be careful not to speak as though there were a definite stock of goods, either of a capital or a consumable kind, corresponding to this outstanding mass of money claims. We can, for instance, conceive of a primitive community with very little Capital, either Fixed or Circulating, but with a money-supply possessing a considerable aggregate value in terms

[1] Marshall, *Money Credit and Commerce*, p. 45; Keynes, *Monetary Reform*, p. 76.

The Kinds of Saving

of goods. We must be careful, too, not to speak as though an increase (or decrease) in the amount of Real Hoarding necessarily implied that Lacking (or Dis-lacking) has taken place.

In conditions of equilibrium, if the Real Hoarding of the public bears a proportion K to its real daily output or income, then K is equal to the number of days in which, on the average, each piece of money comes on to the market in exchange for real income. This conception of the "period of circulation of money," as it may be called, will be found useful later.[1]

§ 4

(4) The last distinction to be drawn is a threefold and a troublesome one—between Lacking which is Spontaneous, Lacking which is Automatic, and Lacking which is Induced.

Spontaneous Lacking corresponds pretty well to what is ordinarily thought of as Saving, and scarcely requires further definition. The definition of Automatic Lacking must be approached indirectly. Automatic *Stinting* occurs whenever an increase in the stream of money directed on to the market prevents certain persons from consuming goods which they would otherwise have consumed. One cause of Automatic Stinting is a decision on the part of certain persons to reduce their money hold-

---

[1] It should be noted that this is not the inverse of the "velocity of circulation" of money as ordinarily understood : for we take account only of occasions on which money changes hands *against final income*.

ings, or as we may say to dis-hoard: another is the expenditure of newly-created money whether by the Government or private persons. Either of these processes brings on to the market an additional daily stream of money which competes with the main daily stream of money for the daily stream of marketable goods, secures a part of the latter for those from whom the additional stream of money flows, and thus deprives the residue of the public of consumption which they would otherwise have enjoyed. Automatic *Stinting* involves Automatic *Lacking* when, but only when, the consumption of those who undergo it is reduced both below what they intended and below the value of their current output. The importance of the distinction between Automatic Stinting and Automatic Lacking will become evident later. Their opposites may be called, for want of better terms, Automatic Splashing and Automatic Dis-lacking respectively. An instance of both has been given in the last section. If certain persons are adding to their money hoards, thus withdrawing money from the market and refraining from consumption of the full value of their output, the quantity of goods becoming available for consumption by others is automatically increased above their expectation, and above the value of their current output.

If *all* members of the public simultaneously dis-hoarded to an appropriate extent, they might impose on one another Automatic Stinting which in each case exactly cancelled the intended Dis-lacking involved in the process of Spontaneous Dis-hoarding,

The Kinds of Saving

so that on the balance neither Lacking nor Dislacking would be done by anyone. Conversely, if all members of the public increased their Hoarding to an appropriate extent, the real income of each might suffer no diminution; for the intended Lacking involved in his Spontaneous Hoarding might be exactly cancelled by the Automatic Splashing in which the Spontaneous Hoarding of his neighbours enabled him to indulge.

Induced Lacking occurs when, the same process that imposes Automatic Lacking on certain people having also reduced the real value of their money stocks, these people hold money off the market, and refrain from consuming the full value of their current output, in order to bring the real value of their money stocks up again to what they regard as an appropriate level. Thus Induced Lacking differs from Automatic Lacking in being voluntary and designed; but it resembles it, and differs from Spontaneous Lacking, in being the direct result of an increase in the stream of money directed on to the market. For some purposes it is convenient to group together Automatic Lacking and Induced Lacking as Imposed Lacking. It will be found, for instance, that the privation imposed on the public by an ordinary process of Governmental inflation consists partly of Automatic and partly of Induced Lacking.[1]

[1] The internal mechanics, so to speak, of a process of inflation are almost as hard to visualize as those of the atom, and seem to require the same kind of hypothesis of discontinued motion. An attempt to analyse them is made in the appendix at the end of this chapter, of which the first section may be read in this place. The remaining sections of the appendix are an attempt to give greater precision to the analysis made in §§ 6–9 of the

Induced Dis-lacking occurs when, the same process which confers Automatic Dis-lacking on certain people having also raised the real value of their money stocks, these people bring an increased stream of money on to the market, and consume more than the value of their current output, in order to bring the real value of their money stocks down again to what they regard as an appropriate level.[1]

§ 5

The expansion of Fixed Capital in a modern community comes about mainly (though not entirely) through the performance of Spontaneous Long Lacking by individuals and corporations. The expansion of Circulating Capital, as measured in terms not of goods but of days' labour,[2] comes about partly indeed through the performance of Direct Spontaneous Short Lacking by entrepreneurs, but partly also in two other ways. The first is the transformation of the Spontaneous New Hoarding of individuals into Applied Lacking; the second is the infliction upon individuals of Imposed Lacking. Both these operations are performed through the banking-system, and they are sometimes exceedingly difficult to distinguish from one another.

Under a régime of mainly metallic money and old-fashioned "Cloak-room" banking[3] the former

text, and should be read in conjunction with them. Induced Lacking belongs to Mr. Keynes.

[1] For the limitations of these definitions and classifications, see Preface 1932.

[2] The point of this qualification will be seen later in § 7.

[3] I owe the phrase to Professor Cannan, *Economica*, Vol. I, pp. 28 ff.

process is easily seen at work. People bring saved money to the banks, and the banks lend it to entrepreneurs, who pay increased wage-bills to productive workers, who on the one hand buy increased quantities of goods and on the other add to the stock of Circulating Capital. Viewing the combined transaction as a whole, we see that the rest of the community has done no Automatic Lacking, for in spending their money incomes they meet with no more competition than if the " saved " money had been spent by its original holders. With a modern banking-system, however, the process of transformation is obscured: for such a banking-system not only itself creates the most important forms of money (whether notes or cheque-breeding deposits), but creates them mainly by way of loan to the business world. By expending these loans business men procure practically the whole of that part of the expansion of Circulating Capital which they are not willing to provide by Direct Lacking. Since the expenditure of new money imposes Automatic Stinting on the rest of the public (§ 3), it is tempting at first sight to suppose that under modern conditions a large part of the new Circulating Capital created during any given period of time is the product not of deliberate "waiting," but of forced levies on the public. On the other hand, since the additional loans give rise to additional money deposits in the hands first of the borrowers and then of those from whom they make purchases, it is almost equally tempting to suppose that the new Circulating Capital is the product of the New Hoarding of the owners of these deposits.[1]

To test the truth of this matter it will be convenient to speak as though the community's money-supply consisted entirely of the inconvertible issues of a single giant bank. We may as well conceive of this money as cheque-breeding deposits rather than notes, since this conception corresponds most closely to the actual conditions in Anglo-Saxon countries; but we must remember that under such a system, while each member of the public is free to alter the size of his individual bank-deposit, the public *as a whole* cannot directly determine the size of the

[1] Some of the pronouncements of Authority on these matters are confusing. Thus Professor Taussig teaches (*Principles of Economics*, Vol. I, p. 357) that "so far as deposits are created by the banks . . . money means are created, and the command of capital is supplied, without cost or sacrifice on the part of any saver." There is a sense in which, as applied to loan-deposits which have not yet been drawn upon, this statement is formally correct: but as an explanation of the whole nature and effect of such deposits it seems, even if we substitute the words "any *spontaneous* saver", to be far too sweeping.

Professor Cannan (op. cit.) flies to the opposite extreme in maintaining (as it seems to me, against all the evidence) that even under a modern banking-system every expansion of bank-loans is necessarily preceded by an equivalent paying in of money deposits.

Mr. Lavington (*The English Capital Market*, pp. 130–3) attacks the difficulty by adopting in rapid succession two points of view. "From one point of view lodgments consist of real wealth and govern loans: from the other the loans consist of paper and govern lodgments." This dualism is suggestive, but I think in the end, in spite of the attempted synthesis on p. 181, unsatisfying.

The key to the whole matter is that the "command over capital" conferred on the borrower by an additional bank-loan is in reality provided, not by the owner of the deposit in which the new loan eventuates, but by some other moneyholder who refrains, whether spontaneously or under pressure, from consuming the full value of his current output.

aggregate of bank-deposits,[1] which lies mainly at all events within the discretion of the bank. This construction, while of course unduly simplified, is, I think, well-adapted to bring out the essential features of a modern centralized banking-system, even where the working of such a system is complicated by the existence of a gold or quasi-gold standard.

§ 6

Suppose first that some or all of the public, their incomes not having suffered any change, experience an increased desire to hoard. Under our assumed monetary system this shows itself, not in an increase of the money total of bank-deposits,[2] but in a diminished daily flow of money on to the market. If the bank took no action, the result would be a fall in the price-level, and an unexpectedly increased consumption on the part of some members of the public, if the New Hoarding is partial, or an unexpectedly maintained consumption on the part of the whole of the public if the New Hoarding is general. By making additional loans of appropriate amount, the bank can prevent these results from occurring. Considered alone, the action of the bank imposes Automatic Stinting: considered in conjunction with the New Hoarding, it nips in the

[1] It cannot, for instance, diminish the aggregate of bank-deposits by buying securities, as both Professor Cannan (op. cit., p. 35) and Mr. Lavington (op. cit. p. 178) seem to imply. Do not joint-stock companies, and those from whom they purchase machinery, etc., keep banking-accounts?

[2] Though if the increased desire to hoard is confined to some members of the public, there will be a piling-up of money-deposits in their hands. Cf. Lavington, op. cit., p. 70.

bud the Automatic Splashing which would otherwise occur as a by-product of the New Hoarding. The bank, therefore, while imposing Automatic Stinting is *not* imposing Automatic Lacking, but is in effect transforming Spontaneous New Hoarding into Applied Lacking very much as a " cloak-room " bank does when it accepts cash from the public and lends it out to entrepreneurs.[1]

§ 7

Suppose next that in a community with a stable population there occurs a general increase in individual productivity. If the bank takes no action there will be a fall in the price-level and an increase in the real value of the public's money stocks —an increase which is a mere registration or reflection of the increase in output, and does not indicate the occurrence of any new Spontaneous Lacking. At the same time the outstanding supply of Circulating Capital, while remaining constant in terms of days' labour, will have automatically increased in terms of goods in the same proportion as the daily output. By making additional loans of an appropriate amount at an appropriate pace, the bank can counteract the fall in the price-level, and, without occasioning a rise, can extract from the public an amount of Lacking—partly Automatic and partly Induced—equal to the increase which would otherwise have automatically taken place in the real value of the public's money stocks. This Lacking is available for increasing the supply of

[1] See Appendix, § 2.

The Kinds of Saving

Circulating Capital as reckoned not merely in terms of goods (as so reckoned it has already increased) but in terms of days' labour. In this instance it is *not* true to say that the bank is transforming Spontaneous New Hoarding into Applied Lacking : what is true is that owing to the increase in productivity the bank has been able, without causing a rise in the price-level, to impose upon the public a quantity of Lacking whose imposition would have necessitated a rise in the price-level if there had been no increase in productivity.[1]

§ 8

Suppose next that, individual productivity remaining unchanged, the rate of total output has increased from a hitherto stationary level owing to the absorption into employment of an increment of population. This implies a preceding increase in Circulating Capital (whether reckoned in goods or days' labour now makes no difference) : and during the production-period (to be called D 1) when Circulating Capital is being increased but output is still unaffected, Imposed Lacking is inflicted on the public, and a price-level higher than that prevailing at the beginning of the period is established. The effect of the appearance of the new output on the price-level will depend on the course of action as regards " saving " adopted by the new population. We may assume that *at some stage* they will set themselves to build up such stocks of money that their Real Hoarding is on a scale commensurate with

[1] See Appendix, § 3.

that of the rest of the population. Suppose first that whether owing to the shortness of the period D 1 or for any other reason they have taken no steps in this direction during the period D 1, but have spent up to the hilt the advances made to them: but that so soon as the new output begins to appear they begin to withhold part of the proceeds of their daily sales in order to build up a stock of money. In this case, if the bank took no action, the price-level would fall, and the Spontaneous New Hoarding of the new population would be counterbalanced by Automatic and Induced Dis-lacking on the part of the old population. By making additional loans of an appropriate amount at an appropriate pace, the bank can keep the price-level from falling, cancel the Automatic Dis-lacking of the old population with Automatic Stinting, prevent the occurrence of their induced Dis-lacking, and transform the Spontaneous New Hoarding of the new population into Applied Lacking available for crystallization into a new increment of Circulating Capital.

Suppose next that the new population succeed in building up their money stocks out of the proceeds of the advances made to them during the period D 1. In this case they cannot properly be said, in accordance with the terms of our definition, to be Lacking at all; for while they have a legal money income they have at this stage no current economic output. What they *are* doing is to reduce the amount of Lacking which has to be imposed on the old population in order to procure the given increment of Circulating Capital and therefore of output. The rise in the price-level during the period D 1 will be less in this than in the preceding case: but in this case, unlike the preceding one, no further expansion of Circulating Capital can be effected through the bank in the *succeeding* production-period without a further rise in the price-level and the infliction of Imposed Lacking.[1]

§ 9

We see, therefore, that even in a community in which (at any rate after an initial rise which we may suppose to have occurred in the remote past) the price-level has been kept stable, the answer to the question (§ 5) of how a given increase in the stock of Circulating Capital has been brought about may be historically a very complicated one: though if we knew all the relevant historical facts, it would be logically quite definite and unambiguous. It remains to inquire into the *rate* at which, without disturbance to the price-level, the creation of new Circulating Capital can be procured through the bank. If there is no increase in individual productivity and no change in the attractiveness of Hoarding, the answer depends partly on the relative magnitudes of the period of production (D) and the period of circulation of money (K),—magnitudes which are determined by entirely independent forces (§§ 2 and 3), and partly on the proportion (q) which Circulating Capital bears to the output during a production-period (§ 2). Put concisely, if K equals

[1] See Appendix, § 4.

qD, a uniform absolute expansion of Circulating Capital can just be maintained with no alteration of the price-level. If K is less than qD, either the absolute rate at which Circulating Capital grows must continuously slacken, or the price-level must continuously rise. If K is greater than qD, either the absolute rate at which Circulating Capital grows must continuously increase, or the price-level must continuously fall.[1]

The conclusion of certain writers [2] that it is the unambiguous duty of the bank to render itself the agent for the procural of just so much Short Lacking that the level of prices is kept stable, seems to rest on too easy an assumption of the fulfilment of economic harmonies. In short periods of rapid change, the incompatibility between a banking-policy designed to promote a stable price-level and a banking-policy designed to secure appropriate additions to the quantity of Circulating Capital may, as will be seen in the next chapter, become a serious source of trouble.

[1] These propositions will, perhaps, scarcely commend themselves without a study of the Appendix, § 5. The assumption here made is that all Circulating Capital is provided through the banks, and that the banks do nothing but provide Circulating Capital. For a more accurate statement of the position, with these assumptions removed, see my *Money*, 1928, pp. 105-7.

It would seem that in normal times both in England and the United States K approximately $= q$D $= 6$ months (1932).

[2] See Lavington (op. cit., pp. 158-9) and Cassel (op. cit., p. 480). These are very instructive passages. The example given by Lavington in support of his conclusion seems to be really an example of the kind of disharmony for the possibility of which I am contending : while Cassel proceeds immediately to admit that in his statement of the case " the unchangeability of the general price-level is regarded as 'normal,' and this is by no means self-evident."

APPENDIX TO CHAPTER V

§ 1

Let M be the stock of money, H its real value, K its period of circulation in terms of finite but indivisible atoms of time to be called "days," T the volume of output per circulation-period, and P the price-level. Then in equilibrium the daily stream of money just purchases the daily stream of output, i.e. $\frac{M}{K} = P \cdot \frac{T}{K}$, or $P = \frac{M}{T}$. And $H = \frac{M}{P} = T$.

Let the Government inflate the money-supply by spending daily an amount of new money $\frac{X}{K}$. Let S_r be the total stream of money on any rth day, L'_r the Automatic Lacking and L''_r the Induced Lacking done on that day, M_r the public's money stock and H_r its real value at the end of that day. Then on the first day we get

$$S_1 = \frac{M+X}{K}, \ P_1 = \frac{M+X}{T}, \ L'_1 = \frac{X}{KP_1} = \frac{XT}{K} \cdot \frac{1}{M+X}$$

$$M_1 = M + \frac{X}{K}, \ H_1 = \frac{M_1}{P_1} = T - \frac{X}{K} \cdot \frac{1}{P_1} \cdot (K-1).$$

If the public acquiesced in this diminution of its Real Hoard, it would spend on the following day an amount of money representing the full value of its output at the established price-level, viz. an amount $\frac{M+X}{K}$. But if, as we shall assume for the present,[1] it retained its old ideas as to the appropriate relation between Real Hoard and Real Income, it will seek to restore its Real Hoard to T. Let us suppose, in accordance with an implicit assumption sometimes made,[2] that it will aim at doing this in $(K-1)$ days, i.e. by witholding on each day $\dfrac{X}{K}$ units of money from the market and performing $\dfrac{X}{KP_1}$ units of Induced Lacking. Thus its expenditure on Day 2 will be $\dfrac{M+X-X}{K}$, and we get

$$S_2 = \frac{M+X-X+X}{K} = \frac{M+X}{K} = S_1,$$

$$P_2 = P_1, \quad L_2'' = \frac{XT}{K}\cdot\frac{1}{M+X},$$

$$M_2 = \frac{M+2X}{K}, \quad H_2 = T - \frac{X}{K}\cdot\frac{1}{P_1}\cdot(K-2).$$

[1] In fact, for reasons to be given in the next chapter, K is likely to diminish in a period of rapid and violent inflation: but we cannot study all the elements in this complex problem at the same time.

[2] The assumption namely that at first the effect of an inflationary process is to raise prices in proportion to the addition made by the Government not to the *stock* of money previously held by the public but to the daily *stream* of money previously expended by it. Cf. Pigou, *Economics of Welfare* (1st edition), p. 672. " If we may suppose the total money value of the country's real income to have stood in any year at, say, £2,400 millions, then the banks, by creating credits to the value of £200 millions, would get command over $\frac{2}{26}$ths of the purchasing power, and so of the real income, of the country, at the cost of making every £ in the hands of anybody else worth $\frac{1}{13}$th less goods and services than it was worth before." Since, however, the period of circulation of money is certainly less than a year, this passage appears to involve the illegitimate assumption that during a process of inflation, however prolonged, the public will never re-spend any of the new money transferred to it by the Government, but will acquiesce in a progressive *increase* of its Real Hoard. See the restatement in Pigou, *Industrial Fluctuations* (2nd edition), p. 151.

Appendix

Thus on this day the Government's gains are derived not from Automatic but from Induced Lacking.

This will go on, if the inflation proceed so long, till the Kth day, at the end of which we get $H_K = T$. Thus the public will have no further motive for performing Induced Lacking, and the following day we get

$$S_{K+1} = \frac{M + X + X}{K}, \quad P_{K+1} = \frac{M + 2X}{T},$$

$$H_{K+2} = T - \frac{X}{K} \cdot \frac{1}{P_{K+1}} \cdot (K-1),$$

and the whole process of Induced Lacking has to begin again.

If Q, the whole period of inflation, $= aK + b$ (where a may be zero), we have, on the last day of inflation, $S_Q = \frac{M + (a+1)X}{K}$, and, on the day after inflation ceases,

$$S_{Q+1} = \frac{M + aX}{K}, \quad P_{Q+1} = \frac{M + aX}{T},$$

$$H_{Q+1} = \frac{M + aX + \frac{bX}{K}}{P_{Q+1}} = T + \frac{bX}{K} \cdot \frac{1}{P_{Q+1}}.$$

We may suppose that the public, finding its Real Hoard now increased above the appropriate amount, intends to Dis-lack to the extent of $\frac{bX}{K}$, and to spread its Dis-lacking over K days. Hence we have

$$S_{Q+2} = \frac{M + aX + \frac{bX}{K}}{K}, \quad P_{Q+2} = \frac{M + aX + \frac{bX}{K}}{T},$$

$$H_{Q+2} = \frac{M_{Q+1}}{P_{Q+2}} = T.$$

Thus equilibrium is restored, and the price-level $P\left(\dfrac{M + \dfrac{QX}{K}}{M}\right)$—i.e. a price-level raised in proportion to the total increase in the stock of money—is a stable one. This is in accordance with common doctrine, and seems to be roughly confirmed by experience.

Thus we do not need to suppose any alteration in the views of the population as to the appropriate proportion between Real Hoarding and Real Income to reach the conclusion that *during the process of inflation* the increase in the price-level is at most moments greater than in proportion to the increase already made in the stock of money. If my explanation of the process of transition from the highest price-level reached during inflation to the new equilibrium level is rejected as fanciful, some other must be given.[1]

If a is > 1, $\varSigma L$ (the total Lacking performed) may be represented by the formula

$$XT\left[\sum_{r=1}^{r=a}\frac{1}{M + rX} + \frac{b}{K}\cdot\frac{1}{M + (a+1)X}\right]$$

If Q is $>$ K, $\varSigma L$ exceeds, while if Q is $<$ K it falls short of, the amount

$$\frac{QX}{K} \div P\left(\frac{M + \dfrac{QX}{K}}{M}\right), \text{ i.e. } XT\cdot\frac{Q}{KM + QX},$$

by which it is often conveniently represented.

---

[1] If, during a period of inflation Q which is $>$ K, the price-level never rose above $P\left(1 + \dfrac{X}{M}\right)$ (as seems to have been assumed in the passage from Professor Pigou quoted in the last note), it would be odd that as soon as the period of inflation is over, it should *rise* to $P\left(1 + \dfrac{QX}{KM}\right)$.

Appendix

Given the magnitude of the total addition to be made to the stock of money, it appears to be true that ΣL will be greater the greater is Q, i.e. the more gradual the process of inflation (this seems to be true even when Q increases from aK to $aK + 1$).

§ 2

(a) Suppose now that, M being fixed, the public wishes to increase its Real Hoard from T to $T\dfrac{(M+X)}{M}$ by a process of hoarding spread over K days, and to that end withholds on the first day $\dfrac{X}{K}$ units of money from the market. Then we have

$$S_1 = \frac{M-X}{K},\ P_1 = \frac{M-X}{T},$$

Intended Spontaneous Lacking $= \dfrac{X}{K} \cdot \dfrac{1}{P} = \dfrac{XT}{KM}$,

Automatic Splashing $= \dfrac{S_1}{P_1} - \dfrac{S_1}{P} = \dfrac{T}{K} - \dfrac{M-X}{K} \cdot \dfrac{T}{M}$

$= \dfrac{T}{K}\left(1 - \dfrac{M-X}{M}\right) = \dfrac{T}{K} \cdot \dfrac{X}{M} =$ Intended Lacking,

i.e. Actual Lacking $= 0$. $H_1 = \dfrac{M}{P_1} = T \cdot \dfrac{M}{M-X}$,

i.e. the public has achieved in one day more than it meant to achieve in K days.

If on the first day the bank injects new money $\dfrac{X}{K}$, we have $S_1 = \dfrac{M-X+X}{K} = \dfrac{M}{K},\ P_1 = P,$

Automatic Stinting $= \dfrac{X}{K}\cdot\dfrac{1}{P}$
= Intended Spontaneous Lacking,

$$H_1 = \dfrac{M + \dfrac{X}{K}}{P} = T\cdot\dfrac{M + \dfrac{X}{K}}{M},$$

which, though less than it would have been but for the bank's action, is what the public intended it to be at the end of Day 1. This is the "transformation of New Hoarding."

(b) If only part of the population wishes to perform New Hoarding, the matter is more complicated. Suppose half the population, A, wishes to increase its Real Hoard from $\dfrac{T}{2}$ to $\dfrac{T}{2}\cdot\dfrac{M+X}{M}$, while the other half, B, wishes to keep its Real Hoard unchanged. Let R be the money receipts of any section of the population on any day. Then we get

$$S_{1A} = \dfrac{M-X}{2K},\ S_{1B} = \dfrac{M}{2K},\ S_1 = \dfrac{2M-X}{2K},\ P_1 = \dfrac{2M-X}{2T},$$

$$R_{1A} = R_{1B} = \dfrac{S_1}{2} = \dfrac{2M-X}{4K},$$

$$H_{1A} = \dfrac{M_A - S_{1A} + R_{1A}}{P_1} = \dfrac{T}{2}\cdot\dfrac{2M + \dfrac{X}{K}}{2M - X},$$

$$H_{1B} = \dfrac{M_B - S_{1B} + R_{1B}}{P} = \dfrac{T}{2}\cdot\dfrac{2M - \dfrac{X}{K}}{2M - X}\left(\text{which is} > \dfrac{T}{2}\right),$$

Intended Lacking of A $= \dfrac{T}{2K}\cdot\dfrac{X}{M},$

Actual Lacking of A $= \dfrac{T}{2K} - \dfrac{S_{1A}}{P_1} = \dfrac{T}{2K}\cdot\dfrac{X}{2M-X},$

Automatic Splashing of A $= \dfrac{T}{2K}\cdot\dfrac{X}{M}\cdot\dfrac{M-X}{2M-X},$

Automatic Dis-lacking of B $= \dfrac{S_{1B}}{P_1} - \dfrac{T}{2K} = \dfrac{T}{2K} \cdot \dfrac{X}{2M-X}$ [1]

If the bank injects $\dfrac{X}{2K}$ units of money, we have instead

$$S_1 = \frac{M}{K},\ P_1 = P,\ H_{1A} = \frac{T}{2}\left(1 + \frac{X}{KM}\right),\ H_{1B} = \frac{T}{2},$$

Actual Lacking of A = Intended Lacking of A $= \dfrac{T}{2K} \cdot \dfrac{X}{M}$,

Automatic Dis-lacking of B = 0.

§ 3

If owing to increased productivity output rises from $\dfrac{T}{K}$ to $\dfrac{T(1+n)}{K}$, we get on any rth day

$$S_r = \frac{M}{K} = \frac{T(1+n)}{K} \cdot P_r,\ P_r = \frac{M}{T(1+n)},$$

$$H_r = \frac{M}{P_r} = T(1+n).$$

If the bank creates new money $\dfrac{nM}{K}$ on the first day, we get instead

$S_1 = \dfrac{M(1+n)}{K},\ P_1 = P,\ L_1' = \dfrac{nT}{K},\ H_1 = T\left(1 + \dfrac{n}{K}\right).$

Presumably the public now wants to increase its Real Hoard to $T(1+n)$, by withholding $\dfrac{anM}{K}$ units of money on each of $\dfrac{K-1}{a}$ days, where a may be $>$ or <1. If the bank wants to keep prices stable, it must now

---

[1] The further history of this case will be complicated by Induced Dis-lacking on the part of B, as to the rate of which it seems useless to make suppositions. B's attempts to reduce its Real Hoard to $\dfrac{T}{2}$ may be foiled so long as A continues to perform Spontaneous New Hoarding.

inject $\dfrac{anM}{K}$ units of money per day, so that on any rth day from the start of the story we get

$$S_r = \frac{M(1 + n - an + an)}{K}, \; P_r = P, \; L_r'' = \frac{anT}{K},$$

$$H_r = T\left(1 + \frac{n}{K}[1 + a(r - 1)]\right).$$

This will go on till Q days have passed altogether, where $Q = 1 + \dfrac{K - 1}{a}$ (if $a = 1$, $Q = K$). Thereafter the public, having raised its Real Hoard to $T(1 + n)$, will spend daily $\dfrac{M(1 + n)}{K}$, so that if the bank wishes to keep prices stable, it must inject no more new money. Whatever the length of Q, $\Sigma L = nT$.

§ 4

Suppose next that daily output increases from $\dfrac{T}{K}$ to $\dfrac{T}{K}(1 + e)$ owing to the absorption into employment, by means of an inflation nM spread over a production-period D,[1] of a new increment of population B bearing a ratio e to the old population A.

(1) If the whole of nM has been transferred to the old population A, we get, on the first day on which the new output appears,

$$S_{1A} = \frac{M(1 + n)}{K}, \; S_{1B} = 0, \; S_1 = \frac{M(1 + n)}{K},$$

$$P_1 = \frac{M}{T} \cdot \frac{1 + n}{1 + e}, \; R_{1A} = \frac{1}{1 + e} S_1 = \frac{M}{K} \cdot \frac{1 + n}{1 + e},$$

$$M_{1A} = M + nM - S_{1A} + R_{1A}$$
$$= M(1 + n)\left(1 - \frac{1}{K} + \frac{1}{K(1 + e)}\right)$$

[1] Assumed here for simplicity to be an exact multiple of K.

$$= \frac{M(1+n)\left(1+e-\dfrac{e}{K}\right)}{1+e},$$

$H_{1A} = T\left(1 + e.\dfrac{K-1}{K}\right)$, $R_{1B} = \dfrac{e}{1+e}$ $S_1 = \dfrac{M}{K}.\dfrac{e(1+n)}{1+e}$,

$M_{1B} = R_{1B}$, $H_{1B} = \dfrac{eT}{K}$, Automatic Dis-lacking of $A = \dfrac{eT}{K}$.

There follows Induced Dis-lacking by A (whose Real Hoard is now too large), and Spontaneous New Hoarding by B. To take a simple (if not very probable) case, if both intend to complete the process in $(K-1)$ days, i.e. if on the second day A intends to Dis-lack $\dfrac{eT}{K}$ and B to Lack $\dfrac{eT}{K}$, we get

$$S_{2A} = \frac{M(1+n)}{K} \; S_{2B} = 0, \; P_2 = \frac{M}{T}.\frac{1+n}{1+e},$$

$$H_{2A} = T\left(1 + e.\frac{K-2}{K}\right), \; H_{2B} = \frac{2eT}{K}.$$

After K days from the start, $H_{KA} = T$, $H_{KB} = eT$.

Now, making the same assumption about the hoarding intentions of B, suppose that on the first and each succeeding day the bank injects $e(1+n)\dfrac{M}{K}$ units of new money. Then, on any rth day, including the first, we have

$$S_r = \frac{M}{K}(1+n)(1+e), \; P_r = \frac{M(1+n)}{T}, \; R_{rA} - \frac{M}{K}(1+n),$$

$$M_{rA} = M(1+n), \; H_{rA} = T, \; R_{rB} = \frac{M}{K}.e(1+n),$$

$$M_{rB} = \frac{M}{K}.re(1+n), \; H_{rB} = \frac{reT}{K}.$$

This will continue till K days have passed altogether. There is in this case no occasion for Induced Dis-lacking by A (whose Real Hoard is established at T on the first day), and ΣL = Spontaneous New Hoarding of B = Automatic Stinting of A = eT.

(2) If B have just done their New Hoarding by the time the new output appears by withholding yM units of money out of the nM units advanced to them, the price-level P_0 just before the new output appears will be $\frac{M}{T}(1 + n - y)$, instead of $\frac{M}{T}(1 + n)$ as in Case (1). By definition yM = eTP_0, whence

$$y = \frac{e(1 + n)}{1 + e}, \quad P_0 = \frac{M}{T} \cdot \frac{y}{e}.$$

On the first day of the new output we get

$$S_{1A} = \frac{M(1 + n - y)}{K}, \quad S_{1B} = y\frac{M}{K}, \quad S_1 = \frac{M(1 + n)}{K},$$

$P_1 = \frac{M}{T} \cdot \frac{1 + n}{1 + e} = P_0$. $R_{1A} = S_{1A}, R_{1B} = S_{1B}, \therefore M_{1A} = M(1 + n - y)$, $H_{1A} = T$, $M_{1B} = y$M, $H_{1B} = e$T. There is thus no occasion for Spontaneous Lacking by B or Induced Dis-lacking by A, and no scope for further intervention by the bank without the infliction of Imposed Lacking and a rise in the price-level.

§ 5

We have to examine the conditions, under various procedures, for daily output to be greater by $\frac{e1}{K}$, and Circulating Capital by C, in each production-period than in the last. $C = q\text{D}e\frac{T}{K}$.

Procedure (2) [§ 4] is clearly impossible if the new hoarding eT required from each batch of new population is greater than the resources advanced to it, i.e. if eT is $> q\text{D}e\frac{T}{K}$, i.e. if K is $> q$D. If K is $< q$D, eT is $<$ C, i.e. each new batch of population spends some of the

Appendix

money advanced to it: thus, in the example at the end of § 4, to the stream of money $\dfrac{M(1+n)}{K}$ proceeding from A + B in the production-period D_2 there is added a stream of money from another batch of population B′, and the price-level rises above P_0. Hence for stability of prices we must have $K = qD, n = y$ (whence also $n = e$).

In examining the course of events under procedure (1), it will perhaps be sufficient to concentrate on the case when $q = 1$, i.e. when the *whole* of each new batch of population is drawn into employment on the first day of a production-period, requiring subsistence immediately, and starting to do its New Hoarding one production-period later.

Assume first that the New Hoarding of each batch is completed in exactly one *circulation*-period from the moment it begins. Then (i) if $K = D$, $C = eT$, and we have, as in the equations at the end of Case 1 in § 4, the requisite Lacking procured in each production-period without a rise in prices by means of an inflation $Me(1+n)$. (Incidentally, in this case there is no reason why n should have been other than e.) (ii) If K is less than D, say $\dfrac{D}{x}$, then at the end of the first $\dfrac{D}{x}$ days of production-period D_2 Circulating-Capital $\dfrac{C}{x}$ has been created. New Hoarding being now complete, we should now have a rise in the money stream sufficient to keep the price-level stable without further money-creation (e.g. in production period D_2 the public money stream would become $\dfrac{M(1+n)(1+e)}{K}$); and to procure by money-creation the remaining $C\left(1-\dfrac{1}{x}\right)$ in the remaining days of D_2 will involve a rise of prices. (iii) If K is greater than D, say xD, by the end of D_2 Circulating Capital C has been created and only $\dfrac{eT}{x}$

New Hoarding performed; and for the remaining $K\left(1 - \dfrac{1}{x}\right)$ days of the "period of New Hoarding" either the process of transformation must be suspended, or in the period D_3 Circulating Capital must be created in addition to that which is "proper to" that period, i.e. which is the result of the New Hoarding of the population drawn into employment in D_2.

If the rate of New Hoarding is slower (it cannot be quicker) than in this simple case, we must look further ahead. Suppose, for instance, $K = D$, but that the New Hoarding eT is complete not in K days from its inception, but in $2K$. Then in D_2 the New Hoarding by the population drawn into employment in D_1 is only $\dfrac{eT}{2}$; but in D_3 there is deferred New Hoarding "proper to" D_2, and fresh New Hoarding $\dfrac{eT}{2}$ "proper to" D_3, i.e. eT ($= C$) in all.

Thus when we are considering a continuous process of formation of Circulating Capital, of which the initial step has been taken in the distant past, the *rate* at which the successive increments of population perform their new hoarding does not matter, only its amount as compared with the requirements for Circulating Capital.

Similar conclusions appear to hold good when $q < 1$, i.e. when, as for technical reasons it is natural to suppose, employed population and Circulating Capital are growing gradually within each production-period (p. 43).

If Circulating Capital is to increase in geometrical instead of arithmetical progression, and New Hoarding is complete within one production-period, we must, in order that prices may remain stable, have $K = qD(1 + e)$ instead of $K = qD$. But it appears that in this case the rate at which New Hoarding is accomplished *does* affect the problem.

CHAPTER VI

SHORT LACKING IN THE TRADE CYCLE

§ 1

We have now to apply the analysis of the preceding chapter to the problem of the trade cycle. From our present point of view, the fundamental feature of the upward swing of a trade cycle is a large and discontinuous increase in the demand for Short Lacking, occurring as the essential preliminary to an expansion of output " justified " for one or more of the reasons set out in Chapter II.[1] Whatever

---

[1] It might be thought at first sight that an expansion of output due to lowered real costs (Chap. II, § 2) would not involve any preliminary increase in the demand for Short Lacking: since the Circulating Capital employed in the industry or group of industries in question, as measured in terms of the group's own products, automatically increases in proportion to the imminent increase of output (Chap. V, § 7). But if the demand for its products is elastic, the members of the group become at once entitled to a greater aggregate reward in terms of goods in general, which has to be advanced to them from some source.

The most obvious and important instance is the increased demand for Short Lacking to carry an exceptionally large harvest of a crop for which the demand is elastic. So soon at least as the crop first changes hands, if not before, and months perhaps before it enters into final consumption, the rest of the community is called upon to advance by some means or other an increased aggregate real reward to the farming population. At the same time the industries which find in the increased harvest a rational justification for an increase of output (Chap. II, § 4) desire to expand their Circulating Capital: so that a double stream of increased demand for Short Lacking is directed on to the banking-system.

may be the case in long periods of steady growth, and whatever *might* be the case in a community of different business habits from our own, there seems no doubt that in fact the supply of Short Lacking is not sufficiently elastic to cope with such pronounced and discontinuous increases in demand, and that the responsibility for meeting them rests almost entirely upon the banking-system. Nor, in view of what has been said about the relation between the period of production and the period of circulation of money (Chapter V, § 9), can it be expected that, even when the new output begins to materialize, the New Hoarding becoming available for transformation should go far to fill the gap. Under such conditions it seems unreasonable to expect the banking-system *both* to ensure that appropriate additions are made to the quantity of Circulating Capital *and* to preserve absolute stability in the price-level.[1]

§ 2

The rise in the price-level necessary to secure correspondence between the demand for and supply of new Lacking is aggravated by several causes.

(1) In the first place, as the price-level rises, even an entrepreneur who merely desires to keep the real value of his Circulating Capital intact will be obliged (whether he be a merchant buying goods, or an employer paying wages) to expend an increased

[1] If the banking-system is obliged also, by law or custom, to preserve a roughly constant relation between the money created by it and its holdings of a particular metal, a third objective, quite possibly incompatible with both the others, is set before it.

daily stream of money. It is true that since his money receipts are likely to be increasing at least as fast as his money expenditure, it will generally be within his power to provide this increased stream himself; but it is at least as likely that instead of doing so he will increase his personal consumption or his permanent investment, and will apply to the bank for an increased money loan to cover his trade expenses. Further, as we have seen (Chapter V, § 2) the hands in which the disposal of past Lacking rests are continually changing,—in other words some entrepreneurs are continually repaying money loans to the banks, and others raising fresh ones. Those who belong at any moment to the latter class will certainly, when prices are rising, require larger money loans from the banks to carry through transactions of a given real magnitude: and while those who belong at any moment to the former class find themselves in possession of a surplus, since their obligation to the bank has remained fixed in terms of money, yet it is by no means certain that this surplus will be placed, either directly or through the transformation of Hoarding, at the disposal of the latter class: it may be utilized for increased consumption or increased permanent investment.[1]

Such behaviour on the part of entrepreneurs necessitates the imposition of additional new Lacking on the rest of the public if the fruits of past Lacking

[1] It seems at all events to be generally assumed that the mere rise in prices, apart from any extension of its commitments, will impel the business world as a whole to demand increased money loans from the banks. Cf. Cassel, *Theory of Social Economy*, p. 391; Hawtrey, *Currency and Credit*, p. 43.

are not to be partially dissipated. If the banks were obliged to scale up the money value of all their assets to the full extent of every rise in the price-level, *no* rise in the price-level could be sufficient, in the absence of adequate new Hoarding, to procure a net addition to the quantity of Circulating Capital. But in actual life the banks have at least one important type of asset, namely, long-period loans to the Government, whose aggregate real value can be permitted to depreciate.[1]

§ 3

(2) The second cause aggravating the rise in the price-level is a lengthening of the period of production, and a consequent increase in the quantity of Circulating Capital required in order that a given rate of output may be achieved. For this lengthen-

---

[1] In equilibrium, let the price-level $= 1$, the Real Hoarding outstanding $= x$, the real value of trade loans outstanding $= u$. Then if u is the bank's only asset, its balance-sheet balances at $x = u$. Let $y =$ the new Lacking required to produce the appropriate increase of Circulating Capital during a trade expansion, $z =$ the new Hoarding done during the period. Then if u must be kept intact it is impossible to find a price-level p_1 such that $(x + z) p_1 = (u + y) p_1$ unless $y = z$. But if, to start with, $x = u + v$, where v is the real value of Government securities held by the bank, a price-level p_2 can be found such that the bank's balance-sheet balances at $(x + z) p_2 = (u + y) p_2 + v$. M, the new money-loans issued by the bank, $= (u + y) p_2 - u$. ΣL, the total new Lacking imposed on the public, may be conveniently, though not accurately, represented by the expression $\dfrac{M}{p_2}$, which $= u \left(1 - \dfrac{1}{p_2}\right) + y$, of which $u \left(1 - \dfrac{1}{p_2}\right)$ may be regarded as going to prevent the stock of Circulating Capital from diminishing, and y as going to increase it. The greater is y, the greater also must be $u \left(1 - \dfrac{1}{p_2}\right)$.

ing of the period of production there are two reasons.

First, if prices are expected to go on rising, merchants become more anxious to hold goods in store instead of bringing them quickly on to the market, and the average period for which goods remain in store is thus lengthened. Secondly, after the rate of output has reached a certain level, physical obstacles and delay, both in respect of manufacture proper and of transport, are certain to be encountered in the attempt to expand it further.

(3) Thirdly, the rise in prices is aggravated by Dis-hoarding on the part of the consuming public. For first, if prices are expected to go on rising, people tend to hurry on with the purchase of goods (such as clothes and motor-cars) of which the exact moment of purchase can be varied within pretty wide limits. The effect of this tendency may be mitigated at first by a more rapid withdrawal of goods from store,[1] involving a curtailment of the period of production and a consequent check to the demand for Circulating Capital : but this mitigation is likely to be soon overborne by the strong forces making, as already described, for a *lengthening* of the period of production.

Secondly, the imposition of Lacking does not hit all classes equally, but bears with especial weight on those whose money-incomes do not respond readily to price-changes : and these classes are likely to seek to evade some of the Lacking imposed on them by revising their views as to the appropriate relation

[1] Cf. Hawtrey, *Currency and Credit*, pp. 42–3.

between Real Hoarding and expected Real Income.[1] As these classes (consisting largely of *rentiers* and salaried persons) are normally large hoarders, they have a considerable margin available for Dis-hoarding without incurring acute inconvenience; and their action may have a marked effect on the price-level.

More important than the Dis-hoarding of ultimate consumers is the substitution of Direct Short Lacking for Hoarding by entrepreneurs, who naturally desire, if prices are expected to go on rising, to keep their resources in the form of goods rather than of money. This substitution is thus in the nature of a direct response by entrepreneurs to their own increased demands for Short Lacking. But it involves no new Lacking on the part of the entrepreneurs themselves, who are merely substituting one form of Lacking for another. The new Lacking done is Imposed Lacking, which is inflicted on the rest of the public quite as effectively by this means as by the creation of new bank loans.

Any cause aggravating the rise in prices directly tends to aggravate it also indirectly by tempting borrowers to scale up the money value of their outstanding obligations to the banks, as explained in § 2.

§ 4

The most obvious weapon at the disposal of the banking-system for mitigating the rise in the price-level is of course the manipulation of its money rates of interest. This seems to work in three ways. First, a rise in the rate of interest allowed to deposi-

[1] I owe recognition of this point in particular to Mr. Keynes.

tors diminishes the temptation to Dis-hoard, and thereby diminishes the aggregate amount of Imposed Lacking consequential on a given addition to the volume of money loans. Secondly, a rise in the rate of interest charged to borrowers has presumably some effect in stimulating those entrepreneurs who wish to keep the real value of their Circulating Capital intact to provide for this out of the proceeds of their own windfall gains rather than apply for increased money loans. Thirdly, a rise in the rate of interest charged to borrowers has presumably some effect in choking off applications for the means to procure new increments of Circulating Capital.

The second weapon at the disposal of the banking-system is the sale of Government securities. The general public, while *ex hypothesi* unwilling to provide an adequate supply of Spontaneous Short Lacking, may be induced by favourable terms to take over a certain quantity of the Unproductive Lacking embodied in the bank's holdings of Government debt. If this Unproductive Lacking is regarded by the public merely as a substitute for Hoarding, it is without effect on the price-level: but if it constitutes a net addition to the amount of Lacking done by them, it moderates the rise in the price-level necessary to procure a given increment of Circulating Capital.[1]

The third weapon at the disposal of the banking-system is the direct limitation, by rationing or other

---

[1] With the notation of n. 1, p. 74, if the public are willing to do additional real Unproductive Lacking $= t$, we get equilibrium with a balance-sheet $(x + z)\ p_3 = (u + y)\ p_3 + v - t\ p_3$.

78 *Banking Policy and the Price Level*

means, of the quantity of new money-loans. In the machinery of direct limitation, the second weapon—the sale of Government securities—plays, under modern conditions in England and the United States, an important and well-understood part.

It will be observed that the weapons at the disposal of the banking-system for checking a rise in the price-level are designed in part to stimulate the supply of Lacking and in part to choke off the demand. About the desirability of the former procedure there seems no question : our estimate of the desirability of the latter will depend on the relative importance which we attach to price-stability as an aim of public policy as compared with other and possibly discordant aims. It is argued in Chapter II and Chapter III, § 1, that, taking for granted the existing state of man's command over economic forces, and also the general organization of capitalist society, certain considerable and discontinuous expansions of industrial output must be

whence $p_3 = p_2 \dfrac{v}{v + tp_2}$. But if the new Unproductive Lacking is merely a substitute for Hoarding, we get $(x + z - t) p_3 = (u + y - t) p_3 + v$, whence $p_3 = p_2$.

It has been impressed upon me by Mr. Keynes that a rise in bank rates of interest stimulates both Hoarding and the purchase of Government securities from the bank, not only at the expense of consumption, but at the expense of subscription to new industrial issues : thus in effect the public is induced to substitute Short Lacking for Long. I do not deny that in some situations important relief may be obtained in this way (a somewhat similar result has been attained, for good or evil, in England in 1925 by the embargo on foreign loans). But the trouble is that in the typical trade cycle, as it seems to me, the demand for Long Lacking is likely to be suffering at least as violent an expansion as the demand for Short Lacking. See below, Chapter VII.

regarded as socially beneficial. It is argued in § 1 of this chapter that, owing to the double function of the banking-system as a creator of currency and a procurer of Short Lacking, it will not as a rule be possible for such expansions to be made except to the accompaniment of a certain rise in the price-level. But it is not denied that for the reasons set out in Chapter IV the expansion of industrial output is liable to be carried beyond the point justified by the underlying conditions of utility and cost: nor that, for the reasons set out in §§ 2, 3 of this chapter, the demand for Short Lacking is likely to be inflated out of proportion to the expansion of industrial output.

It is not denied, therefore, that it is the duty of the banking-system so far as possible to prevent or check these *secondary* phenomena of trade expansion, —if necessary by churlishness in meeting the increased demands for Short Lacking. If the banking-system once loses control of the situation, its attempts to promote equilibrium between the demand for and supply of Short Lacking may ultimately prove hopeless, and there may supervene (as in Germany in 1923) what is described as a condition of "acute shortage of Circulating Capital,"—more correctly, of inability on the part of the banking-system to extract from the public by any means the Short Lacking required to maintain the current or projected volume of output.[1] If

---

[1] In a sense those theorists are right who have found the cause of "crises" in a "deficiency of capital." But what is deficient is not *money*, otherwise the situation could be cured, as all experience shows it cannot, by continued inflation. Nor is there

once this state of affairs is reached, the only remedy the banking-system can apply is to enforce a drastic reduction in the demand for Short Lacking through the liquidation of stocks of goods and the curtailment of swollen productive capacities. It is even arguable that this policy should be maintained for some time after the initial turn in the price-level has occurred. The traditional English policy of breaking as far as possible the violence of the fall may be against the general interest, since it may only serve to preserve in existence a vast mass of " frozen credits," or (in terms of our analysis) to maintain an unduly distended demand for Short Lacking. But it would, of course, be far preferable that the brake should be put on the uneconomic expansion of the demand for Short Lacking at a much earlier stage.

§ 5

From reasoning similar to that of § 1 it seems to follow that an " economically justifiable " decline in the scale of industrial output must as a rule be accompanied by a fall in the price-level. This is true whether the decline takes place from the uneconomic level attained at the height of a boom, or from a level which *was* the optimum level, but has ceased to be so owing to a change in the underlying conditions of utility and cost. And from reasoning

necessarily a deficiency of *goods*, since the available information seems to show that at such times the stocks of goods may be both large and even on the increase. What is deficient is the *activity*, essential to the production and storage of goods, which we have described as Short Lacking.

similar to that of §§ 2, 3 it follows that the fall in the price-level, by setting in motion forces which stimulate new Hoarding and diminish the demands made on the banking-system for Short Lacking, tends to beget a further fall in the price-level which in turn begets a further and "unjustifiable" decline in the scale of industrial output.

It would seem to be the duty of the banking-system to acquiesce in the primary fall of the price-level necessary to establish the appropriate scale of output, and to resist the secondary fall in such wise as to stimulate the demand for Short Lacking through a restoration of the optimum scale of output and length of production-period. It behoves, however, even an advocate of moderate stability of the price-level to admit that it is likely to prove harder for the banking-system to check an uneconomic fall in prices than to restrain an uneconomic rise. For first, while there is always *some* rate of money interest which will check an eager borrower, there may be *no* rate of money interest in excess of zero which will stimulate an unwilling one. Secondly, a policy of direct limitation of bank-loans has no counterpart in periods of falling prices: the assumption made in Chapter V, § 5, that the total magnitude of the money supply lies entirely within the discretion of the banking-system, and not at all within that of the public, seems to have only a limited validity for such periods.[1]

[1] On the other hand there seem to be natural limits to a falling price-level which do not exist in the case of a rising price-level. For instance, with the notation of n. 1, p. 74, if the public, under the stimulus of rising prices, dis-hoard to the extent z, we get

§ 6

The foregoing analysis seems to throw some light on a disputed point in the theory of the trade cycle—the part played by the movements of stocks of materials and finished goods. It is assumed by some that these increase during the boom and diminish during the depression, by others that they pile up during the depression and are trenched upon during the boom. The statistical evidences of their actual behaviour are sparse and inconclusive. There is, however, some evidence that in the recent cycle in this country stocks diminished during the last few months of the boom, increased during the first year of the depression, and during the remainder of the depression suffered a continuous decline.[1]

Our analysis suggests that what is significant is not the actual magnitude of stocks at different dates, but their magnitude in relation to the Short Lacking demanded by merchants and speculators, and made available through the banking-system and otherwise, for carrying them. An increase of stocks during the boom indicates that the increased Short Lacking demanded is duly forthcoming, and is

---

equilibrium with a balance-sheet $(x - z) \, p_4 = (u + y) \, p_4 + v$. As $x - z$ approaches from above the definite figure $u + y$, $\dfrac{v}{p_4}$ approaches 0 and p_4 approaches infinity. If on the other hand under the stimulus of falling prices the public performs new Hoarding z, so that we get a balance-sheet $(x + z) \, p_5 = (u - y) \, p_5 + v$, it is only as $x + z$ approaches infinity, that $\dfrac{v}{p_5}$ approaches infinity and p_5 approaches 0.

[1] J. M. Keynes, *Memorandum No. 1 on Stocks of Staple Commodities* (London and Cambridge Economic Service), p. 2.

being successfully applied to investment in goods. A diminution of stocks during the boom indicates either that there are already difficulties in eliciting the requisite supply of Short Lacking, or that there are technical obstacles in the way of a continued expansion of industrial output, or both. An increase of stocks during the first stage of the depression indicates that the demand for and supply of Short Lacking is being artificially sustained (see § 4 *sub finem.*). An increase of stocks during the later stages of depression indicates that production has not succeeded in adjusting itself to the collapse (possibly by this time excessive) in the demand for and supply of Short Lacking; while a diminution of stocks at this stage indicates that, for good or evil, readjustment of the scale of output has been effected.

Thus the trend of stocks, taken by itself, does not constitute an intelligible guide to banking policy [1]: it must be interpreted not only in conjunction with the trend of the price-level, but also in the light of the phase that has been reached in the trade cycle. During the acute stages of the boom and the early stages of depression, the social interest requires a dissipation of stocks: during the later stages of a depression it requires their valorization; and the loan policy of the banking system should be planned in accordance with these requirements.

[1] This point is well made by Mr. J. R. Bellerby, who distinguishes (*The Control of Credit*, p. 75) between the accumulation of stocks of finished goods in the hands of *merchants*, as a result of speculative activity, and their accumulation in the hands of *makers*, as a result of attempts to keep their plant and labour-force employed in slack times.

CHAPTER VII

THE RELATIONS OF SHORT AND LONG LACKING

§ 1

IN the preceding chapter it is to the vicissitudes in the demand for and supply of *Short* Lacking only that the reader's attention has been directed; nor has any regard been paid to the *composition* of the increments and decrements assumed to occur in the volume of industrial output. It seems likely that some industrial fluctuations, notably the great consumption and " re-stocking " boom of 1919-20 in England and America and the ensuing slump, can be fairly satisfactorily analysed along these lines. But to the present writer it seems at least equally certain that among the cycles of the last half-century the cycle of 1920 was exceptional in this respect, and that on most occasions, in order to obtain a complete picture of the forces at work, we have to take into account the behaviour of *Long* Lacking, and the disproportionate movements which occur in the output respectively of consumable goods and of instruments. Our next task, therefore, is to re-examine, from our present standpoint of the eco-

The Relations of Short and Long Lacking

nomics of Lacking, the phenomena analysed in Chapter II, §§ 3 and 5.

Up to the point at which they reach the hands of their final purchasers, consumable goods and instruments are alike in the requirements for Lacking to which their existence gives rise. That Lacking is of the Short variety, and is provided, as we have seen, either by the entrepreneurs in charge of the production and marketing of the goods, or by the general public under the compulsion of the monetary system. In the case of both types of goods, this Short Lacking is released by the act of final purchase, and made available for embodiment in a further batch of goods. But the purchase of a ship involves a further provision of Lacking, this time of the Long variety, for an indefinite period, while the purchase of a joint of beef does not. Thus an increase in the rate of output of instruments from, say, 100 units to 120 units per production-period requires, if equilibrium is to be preserved, not only a single permanent increase of between 10 and 20 units of Short Lacking, but an additional supply, *in every succeeding production-period*, of 20 units of Long Lacking.

In a community which is progressing at a uniform rate, the new supplies of Long Lacking are provided, as the outstanding supply has already been provided, by Investors. Investors consist of three main classes—private entrepreneurs re-investing their profits in their own businesses, the directors of joint-stock companies dealing on similar lines with the profits made by their companies, and individual citizens purchasing new issues of securities. It is true that the purchase of instruments, in which the act of Long Lacking consists, is conducted with bank-money, and requires on the part of each several investor a more or less prolonged period of Hoarding followed by a discontinuous act of Dis-hoarding; but in a "steady" society such individual rhythms would be merged in a general movement of advance. Long Lacking would not, like Short Lacking, be provided in appearance by the Banks and in reality by the consuming community, but would both be, and be seen to be, the outcome of voluntary decisions on the part of individuals or corporations.

§ 2

It might seem at first sight as if the same could be said of those discontinuous movements with which, in a study of the trade cycle, we are chiefly concerned. Whether an altered expenditure on the purchase of instruments is due to a reduction in their cost or to an altered estimate of the advantage of possessing them, it augurs on the part of the purchasers a rational decision to modify to some extent in one direction their expenditure on consumable goods, and in the other direction their productive effort. The rhythm thus engendered has been examined in Chapter II, § 3, and seems at first sight to need no further discussion in connection with the natural history of Lacking and of Banking. This, however, is not the case, for several reasons.

(1) In the first place, a revaluation of the ad-

The Relations of Short and Long Lacking

vantage of acquiring instruments implies a revaluation, in the opposite sense, of the advantages not merely of immediate consumption and of leisure, but also of Hoarding. This aspect of the matter is especially prominent in the case of the second class of investor specified above, the company-director acting as trustee for his shareholders. Modern professional standards impel such investors to balance up the advantage of acquiring instruments *now* rather against the advantage of acquiring such instruments *at some future time* than against increased leisure for themselves or increased immediate consumption for their shareholders. Thus to a large and probably an increasing extent a discontinuous increase in the purchase of instruments involves a diminution of Hoarding, in other words an increased velocity of circulation of currency and a rise in general prices. The first prices to rise are those of instruments and constructional materials, but the rise is not confined to them. For the recipients of the higher prices for instruments and constructional materials are placed in a position to exercise an increased monetary demand for goods and services of all kinds. Thus the burden of the provision even of Long Lacking is partially placed on the shoulders of the consuming public, with results similar to those traced in Chapter VI.

§ 3

(2) Secondly, since even a single discontinuous increase, and much more a progressive rise, in the rate of output of instruments requires, for the pre-

servation of equilibrium, a sustained increase in the stream of Long Lacking available for embodiment therein, it would not be surprising if the voluntary supplies of Long Lacking should prove unequal to the strain thus imposed on them. This is all the more likely since towards the end of a boom the resources of important classes of investors have been trenched upon by rising real costs of production and by a reversal of the tendency, which marks the early stages of the expansion, for profit to encroach upon wages.[1] While the response of ultimate investors has thus begun to flag, the termediaries by whom a large part of the stream of new capital investment is marshalled—the company-promoters *et hoc genus omne*—may not yet have seen any reason to revise the high estimates which they have formed of the future productivity of instruments. And it is even possible that at this stage the producers of instruments, rather than restrict the scale of their output, should be willing to charge themselves with the responsibility for procuring not merely the Short Lacking required to carry these instruments during their period of gestation, but the Long Lacking required to carry them for some time after their birth. From both these sources a call is made on the banking-system to "provide" those increased supplies of Long Lacking for which reliance can no longer be placed on investors. Now the banking-system can, of course, only "provide" Long Lacking in the same way that it "provides" Short Lacking, namely

[1] Cf. Cassel, *Theory of Social Economy*, p. 594.

by extorting it from the general public through the multiplication of currency. The increasing demands thus thrown upon it add to its embarrassment and may prove the decisive factor in rendering impossible the establishment of *any* price-level high enough to elicit the requisite supply of Lacking (cf. Chap. VI, § 4).

The situation is complicated by the fact that at this stage an appreciable substitution of Hoarding for Investment may be in process. For far-sighted company-directors will be tending by this time to accumulate cash balances out of which they will be able to pay emulcient dividends to their shareholders in the bad times ahead.[1] This gap also in the supply of Long Lacking the banks may be called upon to fill. It is true that it makes no real difference, so far as the effect on the price-level is concerned, whether Lacking is extorted from the public by an increase in the velocity of circulation

---

[1] This is part of the thesis elaborated by Hastings, *Costs and Profits*: see especially Chapter VI. It may perhaps help to account for the curious fact, apparently established by Snyder (*Journal of American Statistical Association*, March, 1924), that in America the velocity of circulation of bank deposits, like the physical volume of production, reached its maximum in the middle of 1919 and had declined somewhat by April, 1920, though in the intervening months prices were still rising rapidly. Perhaps, however, the peculiarity may be attributable to the unusually *non-constructional* nature of the later stages of the 1920 American boom, involving finance by bank credits rather than by the expenditure of balances on capital equipment. In any case, I am not at present inclined to accept Snyder's thesis (see *American Economic Review*, December, 1924, p. 703) of a specially intimate connection between the physical volume of production and the velocity of circulation of bank deposits, for which there seems no logical reason and no corroborative evidence from English conditions.

of existing deposits or by an increase in the creation of deposits by the banks: but the psychological aspect of the latter mode of procedure would probably be more alarming even to a banking-system freed from any preoccupation with legal tender reserves.

§ 4

The upshot of the whole matter is that in a cycle of this constructional kind, as in a cycle of the kind analysed in Chapter VI, the actual "crisis" may be correctly described as due to a "deficiency of capital" in the sense of a deficiency of the activity Lacking; in Cassel's phraseology to an "overestimate of the amount of savings available for taking over the real capital [i.e. the instruments] produced,"[1] in Spiethoff's, to an "overproduction of machines in the sense of a production of more machines than can be sold profitably, since possible purchasers cannot get hold of enough capital to purchase them."[2] Owing to the entanglement, in times of emergency, of the market even for *Long* Lacking with the banking-system, the crisis may occur at a moment dictated by the general state of strain upon the banking-system rather than by the stage which has been reached in the true constructional cycle. It may, that is to say, occur *before* the moment at which the increasing cost of instruments, or the decline in their desirability caused by

[1] *Theory of Social Economy*, p. 626.
[2] Paraphrased from the summary in Mitchell, *Business Cycles*, p. 11, of what is evidently a most suggestive work—unfortunately not accessible in English.

their increasing numbers, would, even if unexhausted supplies of Long Lacking were available, prescribe a revaluation of the net advantage of acquiring instruments and a consequent decline in the quantity of them demanded.

Thus once more, even at this late stage of the boom, the expansion of output in which the banking-system is pressed to participate, by methods which involve a rise in the price-level, may be a rational and justifiable one. It may, nevertheless, be true that the right moment for revaluation of the advantage of acquiring instruments would in any case have soon arrived. When once the crisis has occurred, therefore, the proper policy for the banking-system is, in this type of cycle, as in that discussed in Chapter VI, to damp down the demand for Lacking rather than to improvise a supply. It is only at a much later stage of the cycle, if at all, that a banking policy directed towards the valorization of instruments is likely to be in the social interest.

§ 5

(3) Thirdly, we have to take account of the *complementary* nature of Long and Short Lacking, and of the obligation which rests upon the banking-system to preserve some sort of a balance between them.

(i) Instruments, like other goods, require Short Lacking during their period of gestation; and while the expansion of Long Lacking depends in the main on the initiative of investors, the increased supplies of co-operant Short Lacking have to be procured in the usual way, and with the usual result on general prices, through the banking-system. The pace is set by investors, with their increased offers of Long Lacking; and if the banking-system fails to conform, it will fail to maintain a due balance between the different kinds of Lacking required. Once more, therefore, we find that in practice a perfectly rational and justifiable expansion in output cannot be brought about without a rise in the price-level.

(ii) But this is not all. Instruments require the co-operation of Short Lacking not only for their construction, but for their subsequent *operation*. Towards the end of a constructional boom, therefore, the pressure on the banking-system is increased, and the rise in general prices aggravated, by the demands of the owners of numerous new instruments for Short Lacking to enable them to keep those instruments in effective operation. It is the business of the banking-system at such a time to make the best use of such supplies of Short Lacking as it is still able and willing to procure from the public, rationing those supplies intelligently as between those trades which both use and make instruments and those which use instruments to make consumable goods, and giving a decided preference to the latter. Further, as we have seen in other connections (Chap. VI, §§ 4, 6), the right policy for the peak of the boom is also, contrary to a common opinion, the right policy for some time after the boom has broken. During the whole of the first part of the depression the hands of the banking-system will be full in procuring Short Lacking to co-operate with the *existing* instruments of production. It is only at a later stage that it may be able usefully to crystallize large supplies of Short Lacking in the production of further instruments (cf. the conclusion of § 4).

It is, as we have seen (Chap. V, § 2), an error to suppose that the capital of a modern country consists to any large extent in stores of consumable goods: it is equally an error to identify the "shortage of capital" which precipitates a crisis of the constructional type with a shortage of stocks of consumable goods.[1] It is quite possible that in a boom of this type, as in a boom of the simpler type described in Chapter VI, the stocks of half-finished and finished consumable goods should continue to increase right up to the crisis. But it is possible, nevertheless, that the *rate of output* of consumable goods should be so small *as compared with that of constructional goods*, as to embarrass the progress of the constructional boom both directly by enhancing the cost of production of instruments and indirectly by enhancing the probable costs of their operation and therefore diminishing the advantage of acquiring them. There is, as we have seen, a limit to the extent to which entrepreneurs can transfer to themselves, for retransfer to their workmen, command over the community's

---

[1] As Spiethoff appears to do: and as the present writer used to do (the curious may care to consult *A Study of Industrial Fluctuation*, pp. 170 ff.).

consumable output without endangering a complete collapse of the monetary system and even of the social structure : but other things being equal, the greater at any time is the output of consumable as compared with constructional goods, the less is the danger of that limit being reached.

To a large extent, in the writer's view, fluctuations in the desirability of acquiring instruments are the inevitable penalty of industrial progress : but they are also to a certain limited extent attributable to an avoidable lack of responsiveness in the flow of consumable goods required to co-operate with those instruments in the form of real wages. It is part of the duty of the banking-system to promote at each phase of the cycle such a balance between the different kinds of production as to minimize this source of instability in the estimates made by the business world of the advantage of acquiring instruments.

§ 6

It is worth while to examine, in the light of this conception of a balance of industrial production, some of the remedies and palliatives for industrial depression which have been adopted or advocated in recent years.

(1) Heroic schemes of capital development by public authorities, or quasi-public bodies such as railway and liner companies, have their place in the clinics of the trade cycle ; but there is some danger of their being applied too early and too

enthusiastically. If labour were completely mobile between industries, there would be very little to be said for artificial attempts to annul prematurely the natural consequences of the revaluation which the business world, on the morrow of the boom, has rightly made of the advantage of acquiring instruments. In so far as public opinion has come to demand that maintenance should be provided for indefinite periods for those unable to find work at their customary trades, the situation is made more difficult: for the argument that it is better that shipwrights and steelworkers should make something rather than be paid for making nothing has undoubtedly much force. Even so, however, there is a limit to the extent to which it is wise to promote artificial revival in the constructional trades. It would be rash, for example, to blame the Committee administering the Trade Facilities Acts for their chariness in recent years in extending the benefits of those Acts to shipbuilding: and it is instructive to study the difficulties by which even public authorities are beset in attempting to improvise drastic revaluations of the advantage of acquiring instruments in order to suit the conditions of the labour market.[1] Abstraction made of

---

[1] See the careful discussion by Bowley and Stuart in *Is Unemployment Inevitable?*, pp. 366-77. Mr. Hawtrey's contention (*Economica*, March 1925, pp. 38 ff.) that practically nothing can be effected by a policy of public works which could not be at least equally well effected through an appropriate banking policy, follows logically from his view that "the trade cycle is a purely monetary phenomenon." But it will not carry conviction to anyone who holds with the present writer that the primary reason for constructional depression is a perfectly sensible downward revaluation, on the part of private indi-

the vexed question of human rights, a policy of developing the trades making for immediate consumption would often be theoretically preferable to the practically simple policy of stimulating the constructional trades; for it would ensure that if the other conditions became generally favourable to a constructional revival, its progress is not delayed or prematurely cut short by lack of response on the part of the trades making the constituents of real wages.

(2) This line of argument suggests that certain conceptions of State intervention which are still only in their infancy may ultimately prove more fruitful in damping down the virulence of the trade cycle than the once equally heretical, but now perhaps over-respectable, policy of " public works." It is one of the paradoxes of " private enterprise," with its adjunct of a modern banking-system, that the utmost exercise of thrift and foresight on the part of individuals may be perfectly ineffective in protecting the community from the adverse effects of a " shortage of capital." Individuals may hoard bank-balances and use them later for purposes of investment, but their action cannot result in the community as a whole putting the activity Lacking

---

viduals and corporations, of the advantage of possessing instruments. If this view is accepted, there is nothing inherently foolish about attempts to organize a *collective* desire (say for municipal lavatories) to take the place of a private desire (say for factories) which has temporarily failed. Compare Sir Josiah Stamp's proposals, in his Report to the Restoration Committee of the International Chamber of Commerce, for mitigating the depressing effect of German reparation payments by organizing a quasi-public demand for German constructional goods.

into cold storage and taking it out again as required.[1] Not even the State can put up its sleeve reserves of Lacking to be produced at the critical moment. It does not, however, follow that the State must resign itself to a policy of drift. It may be able to put up its sleeve reserves of those very goods for transferring the current output of which to wage-earners Lacking would otherwise have been required. The discovery that stocks of consumable goods are not the most important form of capital must not blind us [2] to the significant part which they play in the history of the trade cycle, nor to the possibility of so manipulating them as to baulk the cycle-bacillus of his prey.

Considerable interest therefore attaches, in the author's judgment, to certain suggestions which have been put forward recently, mainly by those who cherish affectionate memories of war-time controls,[3] for large-scale State dealings in the primary foodstuffs and materials. The theoretical case for such suggestions rests on the sound basis that the community, acting as a whole, can afford to take longer views than even the richest individual or private corporation, and that with a modern monetary system it is only by actual dealing in commodities, and not by any mere manipulation of

[1] Cf. Cassel, *Theory of Social Economy*, p. 628, " The capital that is used to-day must always be taken from the social income of to-day."

[2] As it seems to have blinded Henderson, *Supply and Demand*, p. 126.

[3] See E. M. Lloyd, *Stabilization*, Chapters IX–XII : and the evidence before the Royal Commission in Food Prices of Sir Charles Fielding (Dec. 31, 1924), and E. F. Wise (January 28, 1925).

Treasury balances, that it can give full effect to those views. If the State could, in the later stages of depression and the early stages of industrial recovery, purchase and lay aside considerable stores of half-finished, or even as its skill grew, of finished, consumable goods, it could promote steadiness not only in the output of these goods themselves, but also in the output of instruments : for by regulating the rate of release of these accumulated stocks it could do something to promote stability in the estimates formed by the business world of the advantage of acquiring instruments, and therefore in the stream of Long Lacking becoming available for embodiment therein.

There are indeed formidable difficulties to be faced, connected with the technique of storage, with questions of Treasury control, with the possible effect on imperial and international relations of Government transactions on a gigantic scale. There is the more fundamental difficulty that to achieve their full object such stocks must be completely removed from the market, and not hang over it in a threatening cloud like the famous San Paolo coffee or the United States Government's merchant fleet. There must be a confidence born of experience that the public authority's resolution is unshakable, and that in no circumstances will it liquidate except at such a time and such a rate as the public interest may dictate. It might even be desirable, however shocking to democratic sentiment, that the extent of the Government's stocks should be unknown, and its dealings in commodi-

§ 7

(3) Of more immediate interest is the question of how far the price-policy of the great combinations of producers of the basic materials of constructional industry—coal, iron and steel, and copper—is, or might be, directed towards promoting stability of industrial output. On this matter two exactly opposite views have recently been given forcible expression. Professor D. H. Macgregor,[1] if I understand him aright, urges that the grounds on which it is commonly held that bankers can check the expansion of industrial activity by artificially advancing the price of loans are equally valid for holding that industrial combinations might achieve the same end by artificially advancing the prices of constructional materials.

"The deliberate placing of the cost of some service in advance of that which the others have reached may . . . create a restriction of industrial expansion, whether the service so interfered with is money or anything else."

Mr. Abraham Berglund, on the contrary, in expounding the price-stabilization policy of the United States Steel Corporation, maintains that

"the stabilization of iron and steel prices, by rendering less hasty the purchases of material on a rising market and reducing the tendency to postpone purchases on a falling market, helps to limit the fluctuations of trade."[2]

[1] *Economic Journal*, December, 1924, pp. 638 ff.
[2] *Quarterly Journal of Economics*, November, 1923, p. 5.

He goes on, however, to point out that such a policy "implies ability to limit or increase output to an extent sufficient to have an appreciable effect on the available market supply," and he proceeds to furnish an elaborate statistical proof that the variability of output has been greater under the price-stabilization policy of the Corporation than it was in the pre-1901 days of unrestrained competition and fluctuating prices. We are in danger therefore of arriving at the conclusion that in order to stabilize output the combinations must stabilize prices, and in order to stabilize prices they must destabilize output: therefore in order to stabilize output they must destabilize it. To extricate us from this logical disaster, Mr. Berglund explains [1] that his measure of output-variability is not well adapted to exhibit the effect of price-stabilization on the general course of the trade cycle, and is largely influenced by brief though catastrophic reductions of output in years of exceptional depression (such as 1908 and 1921), followed by speedy recovery. Such violent changes, he holds, are less damaging than prolonged declines in prices, output and employment. There is much to be said for this view, though it is perhaps paradoxical to describe such a policy as one of "industrial stabilization."

The whole matter becomes clearer if we apply our conception of the distinction between those variations of output (both of constructional and other goods) which are, and those which are not,

[1] *Quarterly Journal of Economics*, August, 1924, p. 627.

"economically justifiable. If there has occurred a real increase in the advantage of possessing instruments, there *ought to be* a relative rise in the price of constructional materials as compared with other goods. If this relative rise is artificially prevented [1] by the great combinations (as by the Steel Corporation in 1901 and the German iron and coal cartels in 1895–9 [2]), the temptations to over-investment are increased, disequilibrium between the different branches of production ensues, and the subsequent depression is aggravated. Since our ideal combination would thus make *some* advance in prices, it would scarcely be open to it to pursue successfully Mr. Berglund's policy of *soothing* consumers by keeping prices low : Professor Macgregor's policy of *frightening off* consumers by raising prices more than is necessary seems likely to be more effective in heading off secondary and uneconomic expansions in the scale of output.

As we have found in so many other connections, the right policy for the later stages of the boom is also the right policy for the earlier stages of depression. If the snake of investment-mania has only been scotched not killed, it is in the social interest that constructional combinations, like bankers, should temporarily keep up the price of their wares (as the German iron and coal cartels did

---

[1] And still more if, the money prices of constructional goods being kept stable while general money prices are advancing, a relative *fall* is substituted for a relative rise.

[2] See Lescure, *Crises générales et périodiques de Surproduction*, pp. 138, 154.

102 *Banking Policy and the Price Level*

in 1900–1 [1] and the Steel Corporation in 1908) in spite of the severe criticism which such action is certain to incur. So far as the Steel Corporation has operated to bring about, with a minimum of friction, " economically justifiable " restrictions of output, and to prevent the recrudescence of over-investment, it seems entitled to the commendation which Mr. Berglund bestows. But there is a real danger lest, at all events in countries which do not exhibit the same phenomenal rate of secular progress as the United States, combinations may, by pursuit of the fetish of price-stability, hamper industrial recovery at a later stage. If the demand for steel has definitely fallen away, and there is no longer any danger of its premature recrudescence, a policy aiming at maintaining the relative price of steel (and still more a policy aiming at maintaining its money price while general prices are falling) will lead to an excessive restriction of output.[2] And a stage of the cycle may ultimately

---

[1] " It was objected that the situation in the iron industry was one of over-production and reckless competition. . . . Herr Kirdorf says that if the prices [of coal] had been lowered considerably, the crisis would have been much severer."—Walker, *Monopolistic Combinations in the German Coal Industry*, p. 236.

[2] If the demand curve for steel (in terms of goods in general

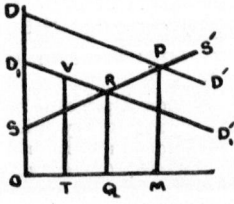

The Relations of Short and Long Lacking

be reached when an artificial lowering of the price of steel, as of the price of bank-loans, below the economic level is required in the social interest in order to overcome excessive pessimism on the part of investors.

Thus it would almost seem that to act beneficially at every stage of the trade cycle trust magnates, like bankers, would have to become infinitely wise as well as infinitely virtuous. If such an event is unlikely, let us at least cherish a modest hope that both classes will grow gradually in wisdom and virtue.

has fallen from DD′ to D_1D_1', the new " justifiable " level of steel output is OQ. If relative prices are to be artificially maintained at their old level, output must be restricted to OT (VT = PM).

Printed in Great Britain by Butler & Tanner Ltd., Frome and London